BASICS FOR
BELIEVERS

For Peter and Mary
with profound thanks to God
for their friendship, example and encouragement

D. A. Carson

BASICS FOR BELIEVERS

ivp

INTER-VARSITY PRESS
Norton Street, Nottingham NG7 3HR, England
Email: ivp@ivpbooks.com
Website: www.ivpbooks.com

First published in 1995 as the first four chapters of a work entitled *Putting
the Gospel First*. Published by Crossway Books, Leicester.

First published in this form 2004
Reprinted 2005, 2008, 2009
Reprinted in this format 2010

British Library Cataloguing in Publication Data
A catalogue record for this book is available from the British Library.

ISBN: 978–1–84474–426–8

Typeset in Great Britain by Servis Filmsetting Ltd, Manchester
Printed and bound in Great Britain by Ashford Colour Press Ltd,
Gosport, Hampshire

*Inter-Varsity Press publishes Christian books that are true to the Bible and that
communicate the gospel, develop discipleship and strengthen the church for its
mission in the world.*

*Inter-Varsity Press is closely linked with the Universities and Colleges Christian
Fellowship, a student movement connecting Christian Unions in universities and
colleges throughout Great Britain, and a member movement of the International
Fellowship of Evangelical Students. Website: www.uccf.org.uk*

Contents

Preface

The four chapters of this book provide an introduction to a letter the apostle Paul wrote to the Philippian Christians almost two thousand years ago. The subjects he treats are so much at the core of Christian faith and life that I could think of no better summary title than *Basics for Believers*.

Originally, these chapters were prepared as four messages delivered during Holy Week 1994 at the Word Alive conference in Skegness, England. I am profoundly grateful for the invitation to come and participate in that ministry of Bible exposition.

Nothing would please me more than if, as a result of reading this book and consequently meditating on Philippians, many believers were to echo Paul's words: 'I want to know Christ and the power of his resurrection and the fellowship of sharing in his sufferings, becoming like him in his death, and so, somehow, to attain to the resurrection from the dead' (Phil. 3:10–11).

Soli Deo gloria.

Put the gospel first!

Philippians 1:1–26

I would like to buy about three quid's worth of gospel, please. Not too much – just enough to make me happy, but not so much that I get addicted. I don't want so much gospel that I learn to really hate covetousness and lust; I certainly don't want so much that I start to love my enemies, cherish self-denial, and contemplate missionary service in some alien culture. I want ecstasy, not repentance; I want transcendence, not transformation. I would like to be cherished by some nice, forgiving, broad-minded people, but I myself don't want to love those from different races – especially if they smell. I would like enough gospel to make my family secure and my children well behaved, but not so much that I find my ambitions redirected, or my giving too greatly enlarged.

I would like about three quid's worth of gospel, please.

Of course, none of us is so crass as to put it that way. But most of us have felt the temptation to opt for a domesticated version of the gospel. In some ways, this temptation is perennial. But perhaps it is especially strong today, owing to a number of developments in the Western world.

First, pressure has been building from the process of secularization. Secularization does not refer to some social impetus driving us toward the abolition of religion. Rather, secularization refers to the processes that squeeze religion to the periphery of life. The result is not that we abandon religion or banish the gospel; rather, religion is marginalized and privatized, and the gospel is rendered unimportant.

The evidence for this development is everywhere, but it can be most easily displayed by asking one question: what governs the national discourse? The answer, of course, is almost everything but the gospel: economics, politics, entertainment, sports, sleaze, who's 'in' and who's 'out'. There is relatively little moral discourse, and almost none that has to do with eternal perspectives – how to live in the light of death and the final judgment – despite the centrality of that theme in the teaching of Jesus. So when we insist on the supreme importance of the gospel, we find many in our society sceptical and dismissive. Unwittingly, partly to protect ourselves from others, partly because we ourselves are heavily influenced by the culture in which we live and move and have our being, we find ourselves formally espousing the gospel, and formally confessing that biblical religion is of infinite worth, while in reality we are no longer possessed by it. Or we maintain the faith by privatizing it: it becomes uncivilized to talk about religion in polite company. We buy our three quid's worth of gospel, but it challenges us very little.

Secondly, the sapping influences of self-indulgence throughout the Western world wield their power in the church. For many confessing Christians, it has become more important to be comfortable and secure than it is to be self-sacrificing and giving. Three quid's worth of gospel, please, but no more.

Thirdly, we are witnessing the rise of what some have called 'philosophical pluralism'. This is saying more than that many Western nations, including Britain and America, are more diverse, more empirically pluralistic, than they have ever been. By almost any objective criteria, we boast a richer diversity of races, religions, moral values and forms of cultural heritage than any of our grandparents experienced. In itself that is neither a good thing nor a bad thing: it is merely a brute fact, one that could be interpreted in quite different ways. By contrast, philosophical pluralism is the settled stance that insists that in most areas of human knowledge, and perhaps in all of them, knowledge of objective truth is impossible. Because it is impossible, it is wrong-headed, and perhaps immoral, to claim that any ideology or any religion is superior to another. Certainly no religion has the right to pronounce another wrong. That is the one 'wrong' thing. The sole heresy has become the view that there is such a thing as heresy.

In such a world, evangelism is easily written off as grotesque proselytizing. Quiet insistence that real truth exists is commonly written off as, at best, quaint nineteenth-century epistemology, and at worst, benighted bigotry. So once again, we find reasons to want only a little gospel: three quid's worth, perhaps, but we shouldn't overdo it.

Paul recognized the insidious evil of similar pressures in the Roman Empire of his day. Like modern Western culture, the Roman Empire had begun to decay. Like ours, it was prepared to use religion for political ends but unwilling to be tamed by it, settling slowly into cultured self-indulgence, proud of the diversity in the Empire and straining to keep it together by the demand for unhesitating loyalty to the Emperor. Pluralism of several kinds made it unpopular to say there is only one way of salvation. Indeed, vassal peoples normally swapped gods with the Romans:

the Roman pantheon took on some of the new gods, while the newly subjugated people adopted some of the Roman deities. That way no god could become too presumptuous and challenge the might of Rome.

That is Paul's world when he writes to the Philippians. He had founded the church in the city of Philippi in AD 51 or 52, and visited it at least twice since then. At this point, however, he is writing from prison, probably in Rome about AD 61. So the church at Philippi is not more than ten years old. Paul perceives a variety of pressures lurking in the wings, pressures that could damage this fledgling Christian community. He cannot visit them, but he wants to encourage them to maintain basic Christian commitments and to be on guard against an array of dangers: temptations from within and seduction and opposition from without.

What a person says while unjustly incarcerated and facing the possibility of death is likely to be given more weight than if that person were both free and carefree. So the fact that Paul felt he had to write from prison to the Philippians to remind them of some Christian basics doubtless worked out, providentially, for their good.

What, then, is his burden as he addresses the Philippians? What is God telling us by his Spirit through these same words two thousand years later?

The first thing this book emphasizes is to *put the gospel first.* It will be helpful to trace this theme in four points.

Put the fellowship of the gospel at the centre of your relationships with believers (1:3–8)

As often in his letters, Paul begins with a warm expression of thanks to God for something in the lives of his readers. Here the grounds of his thanksgiving to God are three, though all three are tied to the same theme.

The *first* is their faithful memory of him. The NIV reads, 'I thank my God every time I remember you' (verse 3). But others offer 'I thank my God every time you remember me', or something similar. The original is ambiguous. For reasons I shan't go into, I think Paul is referring to their remembrance of him. Later on he will thank the Philippians for remembering him so warmly they sent funds to support him in his ministry. But here the vision is broader: he perceives that their interest in him is a reflection of their continued commitment to the gospel – and that is why he thanks God for them.

The point becomes explicit in the *second* cause of his thanksgiving: 'In all my prayers for all of you, I always pray with joy because of your partnership in the gospel from the first day until now' (verses 4–5). Their 'partnership in the gospel' injects joy into Paul's prayers of thanksgiving: 'I always pray *with joy*', he writes. The word rendered 'partnership' is more commonly translated 'fellowship' in the New Testament. What precisely does the word mean?

In common use 'fellowship' has become somewhat debased. If you invite a pagan neighbour to your home for a cup of tea, it is friendship; if you invite a Christian neighbour, it is fellowship. If you attend a meeting at church and leave as soon as it is over, you have participated in a service; if you stay for tea and crumpets afterward, you have enjoyed some fellowship. In modern use, then, fellowship has come to mean something like warm friendship with believers.

In the first century, however, the word commonly had commercial overtones. If John and Harry buy a boat and start a fishing business, they have entered into a fellowship, a partnership. Intriguingly, even in the New Testament the word is often tied to fiscal matters. Thus when the Macedonian Christians send money to help the poor Christians in Jerusalem they are entering into fellowship with them.

The heart of true fellowship is self-sacrificing conformity to a shared vision. Both John and Harry put their savings into the fishing boat. Now they share the vision that will put the fledgling company on its feet. *Christian* fellowship, then, is self-sacrificing conformity to the gospel. There may be overtones of warmth and intimacy, but the heart of the matter is this shared vision of what is of transcendental importance, a vision that calls forth our commitment. So when Paul gives thanks, with joy, because of the Philippians' 'partnership in the gospel' or 'fellowship in the gospel', he is thanking God for the fact that these brothers and sisters in Christ, from the moment of their conversion ('from the first day until now', Paul writes), rolled up their sleeves and got involved in the advance of the gospel. They continued their witness in Philippi, they persevered in their prayers for Paul, they sent money to support him in his ministry – all testifying to their shared vision of the importance and priority of the gospel. That is more than enough reason for thanking God.

There is a *third* basis for Paul's thanks to God for them. It is nothing less than God's continuing work in their lives. 'I thank my God', Paul begins in verse 3, and now adds, '. . . being confident of this, that he who began a good work in you will carry it on to completion until the day of Christ Jesus' (verse 6). This is almost a definition of what a real Christian is. The New Testament affords not a few examples of people who made professions of faith that were spurious, as evidenced by the fact that they did not endure, they did not persevere. For example, at the end of John 2 many people believed in Jesus' name when they saw the miraculous signs he was doing. 'But Jesus would not entrust himself to them' (John 2:24), we are told; he knew their faith was not genuine. A few chapters later, to those who had made profession of faith Jesus declared, 'If you hold to my teaching, you are really my disciples' (John 8:30–31). Or as Hebrews 3:14 puts it, 'We have come to share in Christ if we hold firmly till the end the confidence we had at first.' In the parable of the sower Jesus depicts some who 'hear the word and at once receive it with joy. But since they have no root, they last only a short time. When trouble or persecution comes because of the word, they quickly fall away' (Mark 4:16–17). Speedily they receive the word; speedily they fall away. The most promising of the crop in this case proves fickle: they start by showing signs of life, but never produce any fruit.

Not so the Philippians. Paul is convinced they will persevere, and the reason is that God is preserving them. Paul gives thanks to God because he is entirely confident, as he has observed the Philippians, that God did indeed begin a 'good work' in them (theirs was no spurious conversion), and the God who begins a good work finishes it.

It is worth pausing to reflect on the fact that as Paul gives thanks his stance is not mechanical or merely ritualistic. Look at verse 4: 'In all my prayers for all of you, I always pray *with joy*. . . .' His words remind us of what John says in his third epistle: 'I have no greater joy than to hear that my children are walking in the truth' (3 John 4). Implicitly, such an apostolic stance asks us what gives us our greatest joy. Is it personal success? Some victory for our children? Acquisition of material things? '*I have no greater joy*', John writes, 'than to hear that my children are walking in the truth.' Paul reflects exactly the same attitude. Paul adds, 'It is right for me to feel this way about all of you, since I have you in my heart' (1:7). Probably this was written against the background of Stoic influence that was cautious about whole-life commitments, especially if they involved the 'passions'. Be cool; do not be vulnerable; do not get hurt. But that was not Paul's way. 'It is right for

me to feel this way about all of you', Paul insists, regardless of
what the contemporary culture says. 'I have you in my heart': my
whole life and thought are bound up with you.

Paul's circumstances will not affect his joyful and prayerful
regard for the Philippian believers. 'Whether I am in chains or
defending and confirming the gospel' (verse 7), he insists, he will
adopt the same stance. The clause could be taken in either of two
ways: (1) 'whether I am in chains or brought before the court'; or
(2) 'whether I am in chains or freed again and defending and artic-
ulating the gospel'. Either way, Paul delights to remind them, 'all
of you share in God's grace with me' (1:7).

So strongly does he want the Philippians to recognize his devo-
tion to them that Paul puts himself under an oath: 'God can testify
how I long for all of you with the affection of Christ Jesus' (1:8).
The purpose of the oath is not because without it he might lie.
Rather, he puts himself under an oath so that the Philippians
might *feel* the passion of his truthfulness, in exactly the same way
that God puts himself under an oath in the epistle to the Hebrews:
the point is not that otherwise God might lie, but that God wants
to be believed (Heb. 7:20–25). So Paul: '*God is my witness* how I long
for all of you with the affection of Christ Jesus.'

Here is no mere professionalism. Nor is this an act, a bit of
showmanship to 'turn them on' to the apostle. Rather, it is something that repeatedly bubbles through Paul's arguments. It recurs,
for example, in chapter 4: 'Therefore, my brothers, you whom I
love and long for, my joy and crown, that is how you should stand
firm in the Lord, dear friends!' (4:1).

From both Paul's example and from the Philippians' example,
then, we must learn this first point: the fellowship of the gospel,
the partnership of the gospel, must be put at the centre of our
relationships with other believers. That is the burden of these
opening verses. Paul does not commend them for the fine times

they had shared watching games in the arena. He doesn't mention their literature discussion groups, or the excellent meals they had had, although undoubtedly they had enjoyed some fine times together. What lies at the centre of all his ties with them, doubtless including meals and discussion, is this passion for the gospel, this partnership in the gospel.

What ties us together? What do we talk about when we meet, even after a church service? Mere civilities? The weather? The FA Cup draw? Our careers and our children? Our aches and pains?

None of these topics should be excluded from the conversation of Christians, of course. In sharing all of life, these things will inevitably come up. But what must tie us together as Christians is this passion for the gospel, this fellowship in the gospel. On the face of it, nothing else is strong enough to hold together the extraordinary diversity of people who constitute many churches: men and women, young and old, blue collars and white collars, the healthy and the ill, the fit and the flabby, people from different races, with different incomes, different levels of education, different personalities. What holds us together? It is the gospel, the good news that in Jesus God himself has reconciled us to himself. This brings about a precious God-centredness that we share with other believers.

This means that in our conversations we ought regularly to be sharing in the gospel: delighting in God, sharing with one another what we have been learning from his Word, joining in prayer for the advance of the gospel (not least in the lives of those to whom we have been bearing witness), encouraging one another in obedience and maturing discipleship, bearing one another's burdens and growing in self-sacrificial love for one another for Christ's sake.

In short, we must put the gospel first. And that means we must put the fellowship of the gospel at the centre of our relationships with fellow believers.

Put the priorities of the gospel at the centre of your prayer life (1:9–11)

Already in verse 4 Paul has insisted that whenever he prays for the Philippians he does so with joy and thanksgiving. Now he gives us the content of his prayers for them: 'And this is my prayer: that your love may abound more and more in knowledge and depth of insight, so that you may be able to discern what is best and may be pure and blameless until the day of Christ, filled with the fruit of righteousness that comes through Jesus Christ – to the glory and praise of God.'

This is stunning. Paul's petitions reflect the priorities of the gospel. Observe three features of this prayer.

First, Paul prays that the love of the Philippians 'may abound more and more'. Paul provides no specific object. He does not say, '. . . that your love *for God* may abound more and more', or '. . . that your love *for one another* may abound more and more'. I suspect he leaves the object open precisely because he would not want to restrict his prayer to one or the other. From a Christian point of view, growing love for God must be reflected in love for other believers (see 1 John 5:1). However wonderful this congregation has been, however faithful in its love even for the apostle himself, Paul prays that their love may abound more and more.

Secondly, what Paul has in mind is not mere sentimentalism or the rush of pleasure spawned, for example, by a large conference. 'I pray', Paul writes, 'that your love may abound more and more *in knowledge and depth of insight*.' The kind of love that Paul has in mind is the love that becomes more knowledgeable. Of course, Paul is not thinking of any kind of knowledge. He is not hoping they will learn more and more about nuclear physics or sea turtles. What he has in mind is knowledge *of God*; what he wants them to enjoy is insight into his words and ways, and thus how to live in their light.

His assumption, evidently, is that you really cannot grow in your knowledge of God if you are full of bitterness or other self-centred sins. There is a moral element in knowing God. Of course, a person might memorize Scripture or teach Sunday School somewhere or earn a degree in theology from the local seminary or divinity faculty, but that is not necessarily the same thing as growing in the knowledge of God and gaining insight into his ways. Such growth requires repentance; it demands a lessening of our characteristic self-focus. To put it positively, it demands an increase in our love, our love for God and our love for others.

Just as knowledge of God and his Word serves as an incentive to Christian love, so love is necessary for a deepening knowledge of God. The reason is that it is exceedingly difficult to advance in the Christian way on only one front. Christians cannot say, 'I will improve my prayer life but not my morality', 'I will increase in my knowledge of God but not in my obedience', 'I will grow in love for others but not in purity or in my knowledge of God.' They cannot do it. The Christian life embraces every facet of our exist-ence. All of our living and doing and thinking and speaking is to be discharged in joyful submission to God and to his Son, our Saviour.

So if Paul prays that the Philippians' love 'may abound more and more', he quickly adds, 'in knowledge and depth of insight'.

Thirdly, for Paul this prayer has a further end in view. He lifts these petitions to God (he tells the Philippians) 'so that you may be able to discern what is best and may be pure and blameless until the day of Christ'. Clearly, Paul does not want the Philippian believers to be satisfied with mediocrity. He cannot be satisfied, in a fallen world, with the *status quo*. He wants these believers to move on, to become more and more discerning, proving in their own experience 'what is best'. He wants them to pursue what is best in the knowledge of God, what is best in their relationships with other believers, what is best in joyful obedience – for ultimately what he wants from them is perfection: he prays that they 'may be pure and blameless until the day of Christ'.

For Paul, this is not an idolatrous prayer. For some people, of course, it could become just that. For perfectionists, perfection, at least in some arenas where they excel, becomes a kind of fetish, even a large idol. But this is not the case with Paul. The excellence for which he prays, for himself and for others, is further defined in verse 11: 'being filled with the fruit of righteousness that comes through Jesus Christ'. Moreover, none of this will be allowed simply to enhance our reputations – for sad to say, some people are more interested in a reputation for holiness and excellence than in holiness and excellence. But all such petty alternatives are swept aside in Paul's final constraint: his prayer is offered up 'to the glory and praise of God' (1:11).

That is what Paul prays for. It takes only a moment's reflection to see that all of these petitions are gospel-centred. These are gospel prayers, that is, they are prayers offered to advance the work of the gospel in the lives of the Philippian believers. And, by asking for gospel fruit in their lives, the *ultimate* purpose of these petitions is to bring glory to the God who redeemed them.

How much do such petitions feature in our praying?

When was the last time you prayed that the brothers and sisters in Christ in your congregation would abound in love more and more in knowledge and depth of insight so that they might discern the best things and prove them in their own experience, being filled with the fruit of righteousness, to the glory and praise of God?

What *do* you pray for? Thank God that some do pray along these lines. But many of us devote most of our praying, in private and in public, to personal matters largely removed from gospel interests: our mortgages, physical safety, good health, employment for ourselves or someone else. Doubtless these and countless other concerns are legitimate subjects for prayer: after all, we serve a God who invites us to cast *all* our cares on him because he cares for us (1 Pet. 5:7). But where is our gospel focus? Read through the letters of Paul and copy out his prayers. Ask yourself what it is he asks for. Observe how consistently most of his petitions are gospel-related. Are we being faithful to Scripture if most of our petitions are not?

Put the gospel first. And that means you must put the priorities of the gospel at the centre of your prayer life.

Put the advance of the gospel at the centre of your aspirations (1:12–18a)

The flow of Paul's argument is remarkable.

Apparently some of his critics thought Paul had let the side down rather badly by getting himself arrested. If as is likely he is writing from prison in Rome, he is awaiting trial before the Emperor – and Paul is in this situation because Paul himself has appealed to the Emperor (Acts 26). One can easily imagine the reasoning of Paul's critics. Depending on how this case turns out, Paul's appeal to the Emperor could bring Christianity into bad odour. Paul is constantly rushing headlong into things where a wiser, cooler head would have been cautious. Why did he have to go up to Jerusalem and get himself arrested anyway? He knew how much he was held in contempt there. Surely there had to be a better way.

But Paul has few regrets: 'Now I want you to know, brothers, that what has happened to me has really served to advance the gospel' (1:12). That is what he cares about: not his own comfort, but the advance of the gospel. He offers two reasons in defence of his judgment.

First, his arrest and imprisonment in Rome have meant that the full praetorian guard has heard that he has been arrested for Christ's sake: '. . . it has become clear throughout the whole palace guard and to everyone else that I am in chains for Christ' (1:13). Because the full praetorian guard, when it was up to full strength, numbered close to nine thousand troops, many commentators wryly protest that nine thousand soldiers could not have been cycled in to guard Paul so that all of them could have heard his witness. Surely this must be hyperbolic, or a reference to some small detachment of the guard. But Paul's reference to 'the whole palace guard' probably has a simpler explanation. Paul proved to be such an extraordinary prisoner, and his witness so telling, that stories about him circulated very quickly. It was not that each of the praetorian soldiers took a turn guarding Paul and therefore heard his story from his own lips. Rather, every soldier who was assigned this duty doubtless heard the gospel and perhaps something of his testimony. Paul was neither a hardened criminal nor a suave 'white collar' swindler. Instead of protesting his innocence or gauging his chances of impressing Caesar's court, he spent his time talking about a Jew called Jesus, crucified at the eastern end of the Mediterranean and (if Paul was to be believed) somehow risen from the dead. And according to this prisoner, not only will this Jesus be our Judge on the last day, but the only hope anyone has of being accepted by God is by trusting this Jesus. In short, Paul was proving to be such an extraordinary prisoner that stories began to circulate about him around the palace – and not only stories about him, but the gospel story as well. And that, Paul insists, is wonderful. There has been an advance in the circulation of the gospel because I am in chains.

There is a second reason Paul insists that his incarceration has advanced the gospel: 'Because of my chains, most of the brothers in the Lord have been encouraged to speak the word of God more courageously and fearlessly' (1:14). A whiff of persecution sometimes puts backbone into otherwise timid Christians. Older readers of these pages will remember the five Wheaton College graduates in the 1950s who lost their lives in an attempt to bring the gospel to the Auca Indians. Among the excellent unforeseen results was the very high number of Wheaton graduates who year after year for the next decade or two offered themselves for missionary service. Because of the death of the 'Auca five', many were 'encouraged to speak the word of God more courageously and fearlessly'.

Nevertheless, Paul is a realist. He squarely faces the fact that not every consequence of his imprisonment was rosy in every respect. 'It is true', he writes, 'that some preach Christ out of envy and rivalry, but others out of goodwill. The latter do so in love, knowing that I am put here for the defence of the gospel. The former preach Christ out of selfish ambition, not sincerely, supposing that they can stir up trouble for me while I am in chains. But what does it matter? The important thing is that in every way, whether from false motives or true, Christ is preached. And because of this I rejoice' (1:15–18a).

Who are these curious preachers who 'preach Christ' but who do so out of the most astonishing motives? It is important to recognize that they are not heretics – that is, they are not preaching 'another Christ' or 'another gospel' that is really no gospel at all. As for those who proclaim some 'gospel' other than the apostolic gospel, let them be 'anathema': we would say, 'May they be damned' (see Gal. 1:8–9). The issues are too serious to play around with that kind of pluralism. Those who preach 'another Jesus' are 'false apostles' and must not be given the ear of the church

(2 Cor. 11:4, 13–15). So Paul is not open to commending every preacher who offers some show of piety and who preaches 'Jesus': he wants to know *which* Jesus. We must constantly ask if the Jesus being pushed is the Mormon Jesus, or the Jehovah's Witnesses' Jesus, or the naturalistic, liberal Jesus, or the health, wealth and prosperity Jesus. Or is it the biblical Jesus?

So the fact that Paul can offer these preachers a sort of back-handed compliment shows that they are not heretics, dangerous false teachers. If they had been, Paul would have exposed them. The preachers to whom Paul makes reference here are a different sort: they propound the true gospel, but sometimes do so for the strangest mix of motives. In this case, the people Paul has in mind are those who must be understood to lie behind verse 12. They think that Paul has done damage to the cause by getting himself arrested. Probably they magnify their own ministry by putting Paul down. We can imagine their pompous reflections: 'It really is sad that so great a man as Paul has frittered away his gospel opportunities simply because he is so inflexible. After all, I and many others manage to remain at large and preach the gospel: one must assume that Paul has a deep character flaw that puts him in the path of trouble. *My* ministry is being blessed, while *he* languishes in prison.' Thus the more they speak, the more their own ways are justified, and the more Paul is made to look like a twit.

How does Paul handle this? Is he wounded?

Doubtless he has feelings like everyone else. But he is a man of deep principle, and he perceives that whether by preachers like this, or by preachers who align themselves with the apostle, the gospel is getting out – and that is more important than whether or not he himself achieves universal respect in the church. Not only can he say, 'But what does it matter? The important thing is that in every way, whether from false motives or true, Christ is preached' (1:18), but he can add, 'And because of this I rejoice' (1:18).

Paul's example is impressive, and clear: put the advance of the gospel at the centre of your aspirations. Our own comfort, our bruised feelings, our reputations, the misunderstanding of our motives – all of these are insignificant in comparison with the advance and splendour of the gospel. As Christians we are called upon to put the advance of the gospel at the very centre of our aspirations.

What are your aspirations? To make money? To get married? To travel? To see your grandchildren grow up? To find a new job? To retire early?

None of these is inadmissible; none is to be despised. The question is whether these aspirations become so devouring that the Christian's *central* aspiration is squeezed to the periphery, or choked out of existence entirely.

I recall a Christian some years ago who always gave the same response when he was asked the numbing vocational question, 'What do you do?'

Invariably he replied, 'I'm a Christian.'

'Yes, but I didn't ask about your religion; I asked what you *do*.'

'I'm a Christian.'

'Do you mean that you are in vocational ministry?'

'No. I'm not in vocational ministry. But I'm a Christian, full time.'

'But what do you do *vocationally*?'

'Oh. Vocationally. Well, I'm a Christian full time, but I pack pork to pay expenses.'

At one level, of course, his standard response was slightly perverse. Moreover, in God's universe all morally good and useful work is honourable and not to be dismissed as of marginal importance. Whether it's packing pork or writing computer programs or baking a pie or changing a baby's nappy, we are to offer our work up to God. We are his, and all we say and do, including our work, must be offered up for his glory and his people's good. But having insisted on that point, there are some elements of what we do that are more directly tied to the gospel than are others. Some things we do, and only some things, have direct eternal significance.[1] As the apostle preserves gospel priorities in his prayers, so he preserves them in his aspirations. We must do the same.

In quite a lot of Western evangelicalism, there is a worrying tendency to focus on the periphery. I have a colleague in the Missions Department at Trinity Evangelical Divinity School whose analysis of his own heritage is very helpful. Dr Paul Hiebert laboured for years in India before returning to the United States to teach. He springs from Mennonite stock, and analyses his heritage in a fashion that he himself would acknowledge is something of a simplistic caricature, but a useful one nonetheless. One generation of Mennonites believed the gospel, and held as well that there were certain social, economic, and political entailments. The next generation assumed the gospel, but identified with the entailments. The following generation denied the gospel: the entailments were everything.

Assuming this sort of scheme for evangelicalism, one suspects that large swathes of the movement are lodged in the second step, with some drifting toward the third.

What we must ask one another is this: what is it in the Christian faith that makes you excited? What consumes your time? What turns you on? Today there are endless subgroups of confessing Christians who invest enormous quantities of time and energy in one issue or another: abortion, home schooling, the defence of a particular Bible version, pornography issues, women's ordination (for or against), economic injustice, a certain style of worship, and much more. The list varies from country to country, but not a few countries have a full agenda of urgent, peripheral demands. Not for a moment am I suggesting we should not think about such matters and throw our weight behind some of them. But when such matters devour most of our time and passion, each of us must ask, in what fashion am I confessing the centrality of the gospel?

This is not a subtle plea for a denuded gospel, a merely privatized gospel, a gospel without social ramifications. We wisely re-read the accounts of the Evangelical Awakening and the extraordinary ministries of Howell Harris, George Whitefield, the Wesley brothers, and others. We rightly remind ourselves how under God their converts led the fights to abolish slavery, reform the penal code, begin trade unions, transform prisons, free the children from servitude in the mines. All of society was transformed because soundly converted men and women saw that life must be lived under God and in a manner pleasing to him. But virtually without exception these men and women put the gospel first. They were gospel people; they revelled in it, preached it, cherished Bible reading and exposition that were Christ-centred and gospel-centred – and from that base moved out into the broader social agendas. In short, they put the gospel first, not least in their own aspirations. Not to see this priority means we are not more than a generation away from denying the gospel.

It may be that God has called you to be a homemaker or an engineer or a chemist or a ditch digger; it may be that you will take some significant role in, say, the rising field of bioethics. But although the gospel directly affects how you will discharge your duties in each case, none of these is to displace the gospel that is central to every thoughtful Christian. You will put the gospel first in your aspirations. Then you will be able to endure affliction and persecution and even misunderstanding and misrepresentation from other Christians. You will say with Paul, 'I want you to know . . . that what has happened to me has really served to advance the gospel' (1:12).

So here is Paul's third point: put the advance of the gospel at the centre of your aspirations.

Put the converts of the gospel at the centre of your principled self-denial (1:18b–26)

Once again it is the flow of Paul's thought that is so striking. Paul has just declared that he will rejoice if Christ is preached (1:18a). But that is not the only source of Paul's rejoicing, wonderful as it is. 'Yes, I will continue to rejoice', Paul hastens on, 'for I know that through your prayers and the help given by the Spirit of Jesus Christ, what has happened to me will turn out for my deliverance' (1:18b–19). In this context 'deliverance' does not mean release from imprisonment, but something more important: his ultimate vindication, whether in life or in death. This will come about through their prayers: that is, owing not least to their prayers and the consequent 'help given by the Spirit of Jesus Christ', Paul will be so faithful that he will be entirely vindicated before God in the end. That Paul wants above all else to be found faithful is made clear by verse 20: 'I eagerly expect and hope that I will in no way be ashamed, but will have sufficient courage so that now as always Christ will be exalted in my body, whether by life or by death.'

Thus Paul's driving concern is not that he should be released from jail, or that if he must die he should have a relatively painless departure, but that he should do nothing of which he would some day be ashamed. He wants courage, so that Christ may be exalted in his body, 'whether by life or by death' (1:20). He wants to hear Christ's blessed 'Well done!' on the last day. And he openly solicits the prayers of God's people in Philippi that he might be strengthened toward that end.

Almost as if he feels he must articulate and defend this vision of what is important, Paul summarizes his values: 'For to me, to live is Christ and to die is gain' (1:21). In the context, 'to live is Christ' surely means that for Paul to keep on living here means ministry, Christ-centred ministry, Christ-empowered ministry, Christ's presence in his ministry. To die is to bring that ministry to an end, but even so there is only gain: the ministry is not an end in itself, and it is now swallowed up in the glorious delight of the unshielded presence of the exalted Jesus himself.

What can you possibly do with Christians like that? Kill them? You simply cannot hush them up; Christ means too much to them, the gospel is too central for them. As for Paul, it is not in his power to choose between service here and departing to be with Christ, between living and dying, between being released from prison for more gospel ministry and paying the ultimate price, thus being released into the presence of the exalted Christ. Yet suppose he *could* choose: what would he do? 'I do not know!' (1:22b), he frankly admits – that is, he has no word from the Lord as to what is going to happen and therefore what he ought to choose under such hypothetical circumstances. 'I am torn between the two: I desire to depart and be with Christ, which is better by far; but it is more necessary for you that I remain in the body' (1:23–24) – that is, that he be acquitted before the imperial court and released from prison, and therefore free to continue his apostolic ministry to the benefit of the Philippians and others.

What is striking about Paul's evaluation is how deeply it is tied to the well-being of other believers, rather than his own. Even in this respect, Paul is imitating his Master. 'Convinced of this', that is 'convinced that my remaining alive will be best for you', 'I know that I will remain, and I will continue with all of you for your progress and joy in the faith' – or, better translated, 'I know that I expect to remain and expect to continue with all of you for your progress and joy in the faith.'[2] And even this progress in faith that Paul covets for the Philippians, he construes as a cause for their joy: '. . . so that through my being with you again your joy in Christ Jesus will overflow on account of me' (1:26).

The lesson to be learned is startlingly clear: put the converts of the gospel at the centre of your principled self-denial. Paul's deepest hopes for his own immediate future turn neither on the bliss of immediately gaining heaven's portals, nor on returning to a fulfilling ministry and escaping the pangs of death, but on what is best for his converts. So often we are tempted to evaluate alternatives by thinking through what seems best *for us*. How often do we raise as a first principle what is best *for the church*? When faced with, say, a job offer that would take us to another city, or with mortal illness that calls forth our diligent intercession, how quickly do we deploy Paul's criterion here established: *what would be the best for the church? What would be the best for my brothers and sisters in Christ?*

There is a kind of asceticism that is frankly idolatrous. Some people gain a kind of spiritual 'high' out of self-denial. But the self-denial that is motivated by the spiritual good of others is unqualifiedly godly. That is what Paul displays.

Here, then, is the burden of this passage: put the gospel first. In particular:

(1) put the fellowship of the gospel at the centre of your relationships with believers;

(2) put the priorities of the gospel at the centre of your prayer life;

(3) put the advance of the gospel at the centre of your aspirations;

(4) put the converts of the gospel at the centre of your principled self-denial.

Put the gospel first.

Brothers and sisters in Christ, such a valuation of the gospel ought not to be the exception among us, but the rule. We are talking about the good news that reconciles lost men and women to the eternal God. We are confessing the gospel: that God himself has provided a redeemer who died, the just for the unjust, to bring us to himself. Without this gospel we are cut off, without hope in this world or the next, utterly undone. Compared with this good news, what could possibly compete? Put the gospel first.

One remembers what an ageing Christian said to John G. Paton in the nineteenth century when Paton was planning to go as a missionary to the South Sea Islands. 'You'll be eaten by cannibals,' Paton was warned.

Paton replied, 'Mr. Dickson, you are advanced in years now and your own prospect is soon to be laid in the grave, there to be eaten by worms; I confess to you, that if I can but live and die serving and honouring the Lord Jesus, it will make no difference to me whether I am eaten by cannibals or by worms; and in the Great Day my resurrection body will arise as fair as yours in the likeness of our risen Redeemer.'[3]

Put the gospel first. 'Only one life, 'twill soon be passed; Only what's done for Christ will last.'

Put the gospel first.

2

Adopt Jesus' death as a test of your outlook

Philippians 1:27 – 2:18

What does the cross achieve? Why does it occupy so central a place in the minds of the New Testament writers?

The Bible gives many wonderfully rich answers to such questions. I would like to begin this chapter by sketching a few of them. It will prove helpful to think about the cross from various perspectives, before we examine exactly what the passage before us has to contribute to a comprehensive theology of the cross.

God's perspective

What does the cross look like to God?

If we ask that question of contemporary writers, immediately we are embroiled in various disputes, even a dispute about the translation of a word. Perhaps it will clarify the issues a little if we lightly trace out one such argument.

According to 1 John 2:2, believers have an Advocate with the Father, Jesus Christ, the Righteous One. And he (according to the Authorized Version) is the 'propitiation' for our sins. What does that mean? The NIV declares that Jesus is the 'atoning sacrifice' for our sins. What does this change in wording signify? The issue is crucially important if we are to grasp how God views the cross.

'Propitiation' is that act by which God becomes 'propitious', that is, favourable. For centuries the church happily used the term. The cross is the place, the event, the sacrifice, by which God becomes favourable or propitious to us poor sinners. The cross, in other words, was the place of propitiation; it was the means by which God was propitiated, his anger assuaged and appeased. But about seventy years ago it became out of vogue to speak of propitiation. The argument went something like this. 'Propitiation' sounds too much like pagan sacrifice. In animistic cultures, the aim of many of the sacrifices offered to various spirits and deities is to win their approval – in short, to propitiate them. You don't want the storm gods to be angry. You certainly want the appropriate deity to ensure that the crops will be good, or that your wife has a fat baby, or that your husband comes home safely from his hunting expedition in the jungle. So you offer the spirits the prescribed sacrifices and thereby try to win their favour. You are performing an act of propitiation. In this model, human beings are the subjects, and they propitiate the gods, who are the objects of this action.

But if that model prevails, it was argued, how can one reasonably think of the cross as an act of propitiation? In the cross, human beings do not offer up a sacrifice to appease God. Far from it: God himself is the subject, the one who loves the world so much as to send his Son (John 3:16). He initiates the action; he sends his own Son to be the sacrifice. So how can the sacrifice propitiate him, when he initiated the act of sacrifice? So we must not think of the cross as an act of *propitiation*, but as an act of *expiation* – that is, the cross has nothing to do with making God favourable (since God is already so favourable to this broken world that he has sent his beloved Son), and has everything to do with cancelling sin.

No sooner was this argument put forth than objections appeared. How can we dispense with the notion of propitiation, in the light of the many biblical passages that speak of the wrath of God? If God is wrathful on account of our sin, if he is truly angry, then that which removes his anger is that which propitiates him. In other words, we cannot get away from the notion of propitiation as long as the Bible talks about the wrath of God. It is a fearful thing to fall under that wrath. What sets aside that wrath is the cross: Jesus takes our punishment, and we go free. Propitiation must not be set aside.

The new voices replied to the effect that the only way we can reconcile passages that speak of the wrath of God with passages that tell us that God loved the world so much that he sent his Son is by recognizing that the 'wrath' of God must be understood in impersonal terms. In this view, the 'wrath of God' is merely a metaphorical way of talking about the terrible yet inevitable results of sin. If you do bad things, bad things ensue. That is the way God has constructed the universe: in that sense, the bad things that follow your evil can be traced, however indirectly, to God. But God himself, they argued, cannot be thought of as personally angry: how could that be, when this God, in love, sent his Son while we were yet sinners?

But the traditional voices would not be silenced. The new view that wants to ban propitiation simply does not take sin and wrath seriously enough. It is not true that doing bad things always works out in impersonal judgment: sometimes wicked people get away with horrible sins, and even prosper because of them. Unless one holds that God personally responds in judgment to balance the books, it is terribly naïve to think that impersonal judgment prevails with justice. Besides, in the few places in the Bible where the word traditionally rendered 'propitiation' is found, the surrounding context is, repeatedly, the wrath of God. Granted this link, how can one responsibly say that God's wrath is nothing more than the inevitable *and impersonal* outworking of evil? As soon argue that the love of God is also impersonal, and nothing more than the inevitable outworking of good! The entire conception of God is drifting from biblical theism to thoroughly unbiblical deism.

And so the debate goes on. A lot of ink has been spilled on this question. But some of that debate is misguided, because it attempts to drive wedges between truths that the Bible joins together. In particular, the Bible insists that God is simultaneously angry and loving. What the Bible says about propitiation cannot be grasped unless this point is understood.

In the Bible, God's wrath is a function of his holiness. His wrath or anger is not the explosion of a bad temper, of a chronic inability to restrain his irritability, but of just and principled opposition to sin. God's holiness is so spectacularly glorious that it *demands* that he be wrathful with those of his creatures who defy him, slight his majesty, thumb their noses at his words and works, and insist on their own independence when every breath they breathe, not to say their very existence, depends on his providential care. If God were to gaze at sin and rebellion, shrug his shoulders, and mutter, 'Well, I'm not too bothered. I can forgive these people. I don't really care what they do', surely there would be something morally deficient about him. Should God care nothing for Hitler's outrages? Should God care nothing about my rebellion and your rebellion? If he acted this way, he would ultimately discount his own significance, sully his own glory, besmirch his own honour, and soil his own integrity.

That is why, in Scripture, God is sometimes portrayed as blisteringly angry. Moreover, it is important that we reject the common evangelical cliché on this subject: 'God hates the sin but loves the sinner.' The second part may be true, but, as cast, this antithesis is fundamentally mistaken, and is clearly refuted by Scripture. For example, fourteen times in the first fifty psalms alone the texts insist that God 'hates' sinners, 'abhors' those who tell lies, and so forth.

But the glorious truth about God is that although he is angry with us, in his very character he is a God of love. Despite his anger as he perceives our anarchy, anger that is a necessary function of his holiness, God is a loving God, and so he provides a means of forgiving sins *that will leave the integrity of his glory unsullied.* He comes to us in the person of his Son. His Son dies as the propitiation of our sins: that is, he dies to ensure that God becomes favourable toward us in precisely those areas where God has been standing over against us in judgment and wrath. But because God himself is the One who has provided the sacrifice, this is quite unlike pagan propitiation. In pagan propitiation, as we have seen, *we* offer the sacrifices and the gods are propitiated. By contrast, in the Bible God is both the origin and the object of the propitiating sacrifice. He provides it by sending his Son to the cross; at the same time, the sacrifice satisfies God's own honour, and his righteous wrath is turned away without his holiness being impugned.

Much of this is summarized in another letter written by Paul: 'God presented Jesus as a propitiation [NIV 'sacrifice of atonement'] in his blood. He did this to demonstrate his justice, because in his forbearance he had left the sins committed beforehand unpunished – he did it to demonstrate his justice at the present time, so as to be just and the one who justifies those who have faith in Jesus' (Rom. 3:25–26). Observe how Paul repeatedly insists that God sent his Son to the cross 'to demonstrate his justice' – not simply to save us, but *to demonstrate his justice,* as well as to be the

One who justifies those who have faith in his Son. It is the cross that unites God's love and his perfect holiness.

Sometimes poetry says this better than prose:

Love in the Deity stretches conceptions of men;
Love seems not love which permits our full measure of
    hate.
Promise of judgment in ages beyond seems too late.
Where is God's love when the wretched are wretched
    again?
Holiness absolute stands far removed from our ken,
Either its brightness so alien it seems to frustrate,
Blindingly brilliant, or else its rich glories abate,
Fading in mist as the distance seems too much to mend.
    One place remains where this love and this holiness meet,
    Mingling in poetic measures with no verbal dross.
    Symbol of holiness pure, justice without defeat,
    Coupled with unbounded love, stands the stark, ugly
        cross.

Lord God of hosts, in the worship surrounding your throne
Questions once clamouring give place to hushed homage
    alone.

That is one of the ways, at least, that God looks at the cross.

Christ's perspective

Here, too, many things could be said. But one of the great and neglected themes about what the cross means to the Son is the obedience of the Son. This theme surfaces with special strength in the epistle to the Hebrews and in the gospel of John. There we repeatedly learn that the Father sends and the Son goes; the Father commissions and the Son obeys. The Son always does what pleases the Father (John 8:29). The most staggering commission the Father gives to the Son is to go to the cross to redeem a race of rebels. And the Son knows that that is the commission given him: Jesus came, he insists, not to be served, but to serve, and to give his life as a ransom for many (Mark 10:45). But knowledge of the commission he had received did not make obedience easy: Gethsemane and the cross were faced with an agony of intercession, characterized by the repeated petition, 'Yet not what I will but what you will' (Mark 14:36).

Thus the cross for Jesus was not only the means by which he sacrificed himself, the just for the unjust, to bring us to God, but also the high point of his unqualified obedience to his heavenly Father. That point is alluded to in the passage before us: 'And being found in appearance as a man, he humbled himself and became *obedient* to death – even death on a cross!' (2:8).

The devil's perspective

One of the most important chapters in the New Testament for understanding the devil's perspective on the cross is Revelation 12. There Satan is portrayed as full of rage because he has been banished from heaven and knows that his time is short. He has not been able to crush Jesus, so he vents his rage on the church. He is the 'accuser of the brothers' who simultaneously wants to vex their consciences and accuse God of ungodliness because he, God, accepts such miserable sinners as these. But believers, we are told, defeat Satan on the ground of 'the blood of the Lamb' – an unambiguous reference to the cross. What does this mean?

What is meant, of course, is that these believers escape the accusations of Satan himself, whether in their own minds and consciences or before the bar of God's justice, because they make instant appeal to the cross. They sing with full attention and deep gratitude the wonderful words,

Nothing in my hands I bring,
Simply to thy cross I cling.

Before that appeal, Satan has no retort. God *has* retained his honour while redeeming a rebel brood. We *can* be free from guilt – both objective guilt before a holy God and subjective awareness of guilt – not because we ourselves are guiltless but because Jesus 'himself bore our sin in his body on the tree, so that we might die to sins and live for righteousness; by his wounds you have been healed' (1 Pet. 2:24).

Imagine the first Passover, just before the exodus. Mr Smith and Mr Jones, two Hebrews with remarkable names, are discussing the extraordinary events of the previous weeks and months. Mr Smith asks Mr Jones, 'Have you sprinkled the blood of a lamb on the two doorposts and on the lintel over the entrance to your dwelling?'

'Of course', replies Mr Jones. 'I've followed Moses' instructions exactly.'

'So have I', affirms Mr Smith. 'But I have to admit I'm very nervous. My boy Charlie means the world to me. If the angel of death passes through the land tonight, as Moses says, taking out all the firstborn in the land, I just don't know what I'll do if Charlie dies.'

'But that's the point. He won't die. That's why you sprinkled the lamb's blood on the doorposts and on the lintel. Moses said that when the angel of death sees the blood, he will "pass over" the house so protected, and the firstborn will be safe. Why are you worried?'

'I know, I know', splutters Mr Smith, somewhat irritably. 'But you have to admit that there have been some very strange goings-on these last few months. Some of the plagues have afflicted only the Egyptians, of course, but some of them have hit us, too. The thought that my Charlie could be in danger is terribly upsetting.'

Rather unsympathetically, Mr Jones replies, 'I really can't imagine why you're fretting. After all, I have a son, too, and I think I love him just as much as you love your Charlie. But I am completely at peace: God promised that the angel of death would pass over every house whose door is marked by blood in the way he prescribes, and I take him at his word.'

That night the angel of death passed through the land. Who lost his son, Mr Smith or Mr Jones?

The answer, of course, is – neither. For God's promise that the angel of death would simply 'pass over' and not destroy was not made conditional on the intensity of the faith of the residents, but only on whether or not they had sprinkled blood on the doorposts and on the lintel. In both cases the blood was shed, the houses marked; in both cases the firstborn son was saved.

So with us, who have come to trust Christ and his cross-work on our behalf. The promise of deliverance, the assurance that we are accepted by almighty God, is not tied to the intensity of our faith, or to the consistency of our faith, or to the purity of our faith, but to the object of our faith. When we approach God in prayer, our plea is not that we have been good that day, or that we have just come from a Christian meeting full of praise, or that we try harder, but that Christ has died for us. And against that plea, Satan has no riposte.

For the truth of the matter is that the cross marks Satan's defeat. And Satan knows it. That is what the cross means to him.

Sin's perspective

Sin is not a living thing, of course; one cannot suppose that sin literally has a perspective. But the category is useful, even if metaphorical, because it helps us see what the cross achieved with respect to sin.

The answer to that question is highly diverse in the Bible, because sin can be thought of in so many ways. Sin can be thought of as a debt: I owe something I cannot pay. In that case the cross is seen as the means by which the debt is paid. One sometimes reads on Christmas cards the two-line poem,

> He came to pay a debt he did not owe
> Because we owed a debt we could not pay.

That is exactly right. That is what the cross achieved.

Sin can also be thought of as a stain. In that case the dirt is removed by the death of Christ. Or sin is offence before God. In that case we insist that the cross expiates our sin, it cancels it and thus removes it. Regardless, however, of what foul imagery is used to depict odious sin, the cross is the solution, the sole solution.

Our perspective

Here, too, many complementary things could be underlined. The cross is the high-water mark of the demonstration of God's love for his people. It is a symbol of our shame, and of our freedom. It is the ultimate measure of how serious our guilt is, and the comforting assurance that our guilt has been dealt with. In the New Testament, the cross is tied to many of the most important words and concepts: justification, sanctification, the gift of the Spirit, the dawning of the kingdom.

But in the New Testament the cross also serves as the supreme standard of our behaviour. That theme is perhaps most dramatically drawn, in the New Testament, by the apostle Peter in his first letter. But it is also the primary point that Paul makes here: 'Your attitude should be the same as that of Christ Jesus', Paul writes (2:5) – and then he presses on to the cross.[4]

Although the passage before us runs from 1:27 to 2:18, there is little doubt that the core section is 2:6–11. We shall see not only that it is important for what it says about Jesus and his cross, but that its thought controls the surrounding paragraphs.

There is at least some evidence, albeit disputed, that this passage preserves some early Christian hymn. That is why the NIV sets out the text in poetic lines. Some have criticized these lines because in Greek they do not seem to scan as poetry very well. One remembers the limerick:

There once was a poet from Japan
Whose poems could not possibly scan.
    When told this was so,
    He replied, 'Yes, I know;
That is because I always try to squeeze as many words into
    the last line as I possibly can.'

It would be unfair to accuse Paul of this particular deviation. But one must remember that Greek poetry, like its contemporary English counterpart, can break forms for the sake of effect.

It is possible that this hymn (if hymn it be) is older than the letter to the Philippians, and that just as Paul quotes the Old Testament (and on occasion can even quote pagan lines), so there is no reason why he should not here draw on some hymn of the church. If that is what Paul has done, he may also have adapted it.

Alternatively, he may have written the entire passage himself (just as I have sometimes written poetry to illustrate or adorn some prose piece I have written). Either way, by deploying these lines here, they have been preserved in an apostolic writing judged canonical, and thus have come down to us for our edification.

This great passage can most usefully be broken down into two parts.

Verses 6–8

Verse 5 tells us that our attitude should be the same as that of Christ Jesus, whose attitude in his own indescribably remarkable self-denial is the theme of the first part of this passage. 'Being in very nature God, [he] did not consider equality with God something to be grasped': there are two important elements to understanding these opening words. First, the words 'being in very nature God', more literally 'being in the *form* of God', do not precisely address the distinction between essence and function much loved in the Western world. The passage is not quite saying that he was in very essence God, still less that he merely functioned as if he were God (which would surely be a shocking thing to say anyway, granted who the God of the Bible is). The word used is a subtle shading of both ideas. In the next verse it appears again: Jesus empties himself and takes 'the very nature of a servant', more literally 'the *form* of a servant' (2:8). Clearly in this latter context it is not merely ontology, mere essence, mere being, that is being claimed: Jesus lives and acts and functions as a servant.

The idea, then, is that Christ Jesus began, shall we say, in the mode of existence of God himself, but took on the mode of existence of a servant. This 'mode of existence' of God embraces both essence and function: he enjoyed real equality with God, and he becomes a real servant. That is why the second line of verse 6 insists that Jesus 'did not consider equality with God something to be grasped', or, perhaps, better, something to be exploited, something to be deployed for his own advantage. Rather, he 'made himself nothing' and took 'the mode of existence of a servant'.

Secondly, the opening expression, both in Greek and in English, is slightly ambiguous: *'being* in very nature God' could be understood in one of two ways. It could be understood concessively: *'although* he was in very nature God', he took on the form of a servant. Or it could be understood causally: *'because* he was in very nature God', he took on the form of a servant. On the whole, the latter better suits the context. The eternal Son did not think of his status as God as something which gave him the opportunity to get and get and get. Instead, his very status as God meant he had nothing to prove, nothing to achieve. And precisely because he is one with God, one with this kind of God, he 'made himself nothing', and gave and gave and gave.

He 'made himself nothing': What does that mean? Literally translated, the original reads, 'He emptied himself.' But the expression does not mean he emptied himself *of something.* For example, it is not as if he emptied himself of his deity, for then he would not longer be God. Nor did he empty himself of the attributes of his deity (though that has been argued), for the result would be the same. An animal that waddles like a porcupine, and has the quills of a porcupine, and in general all the attributes of a porcupine, is a porcupine. If you take away all the attributes of a porcupine, whatever you have left is not a porcupine. Likewise, if the Son is stripped of the attributes of deity, it is difficult to see how he can in any meaningful sense still claim to be deity.

In fact, the expression 'he emptied himself', far from meaning he emptied himself *of something,* is idiomatic for 'he gave up all his rights' or the like. He emptied *himself;* hence NIV's '[he] made himself nothing' – not literally nothing, of course, for then he would not be here. He abandoned his rights; he became a nobody. In particular, Paul tells us in the next line that Jesus became a servant, a slave. That is of course the defining characteristic of slaves: from many points of view, they are nobodies. They might represent certain wealth to their owners, and they might have certain cherished skills. But they have no rights; they are nobodies. By contrast, the eternal Son has always had all the rights of deity; he was one with God. But precisely because of this, he did not perceive his equality with God something to be exploited, but became a nobody. He 'made himself nothing, taking the very nature of a slave'.

It is important to recognize that Paul does not tell us that Christ exchanged one form for another. Paul is not saying that Jesus was God, gave that up, and became a slave instead. Rather, without ever abandoning who he is, he adopts the mode of exist-ence of a slave. To do this, he (literally) becomes 'in human likeness' (2:7): the idea is not that he merely becomes *like* a human being, a reasonable facsimile but not truly human. Rather, it means that he becomes a being fashioned in this way – a human being. He was always God; he now becomes something he was not, a human being. 'And being found in appearance as a man, he humbled himself and became obedient to death – even death on a cross!' (2:8).

It is very hard for us today to hear the shocking overtones of the words Paul uses, because the cross has become for us such a domesticated symbol. Today many women and some men dangle crosses from their ears. Our bishops hang crosses around their necks. Our buildings have crosses on the spires, or stained wooden crosses are backlit with fluorescent lights. Some of our older church buildings are actually built in cruciform, and no-one is shocked.

Suppose you were to place in a prominent position in your church building a fresco of the massed graves of Auschwitz. Would not everyone be horrified? But in the first century, the cross had something of that symbolic value. Scholars have gone through every instance of the word 'cross' and related expressions that have come down to us from about the time of Jesus, and shown how 'crucifixion' and 'cross' inevitably evoke horror. Of the various forms of Roman execution, crucifixion could be used only for slaves, rebels and anarchists; it could never be used for a Roman citizen, unless with the express sanction of the Emperor. Crucifixion was considered too cruel – so shameful that the word itself was avoided in polite conversation.

But here is Paul, bold as brass, insisting that the Lord Christ whom we serve, precisely because he is that kind of God, makes himself a nobody, becomes in fact a slave (becoming a human being as part of this process), and then humbles himself yet further and obeys his heavenly Father by dying – by dying the odious, revolting death of the cross, reserved for public enemies and the dregs of the criminal justice system. The language is *meant* to shock. Jesus died on a *cross*!

I believe it was W. H. Auden who penned the lines,

Only the unscarred, overfed,
Enjoy the verbal event of Calvary.

Verses 9–11

The second part of this 'hymn' (if hymn it be) treats the Son's vindication. 'Therefore', Paul writes – because of his self-emptying, because of his obedience, because of his death on the cross – therefore 'God exalted him to the highest place and gave him the name that is above every name, that at the name of Jesus every knee should bow, in heaven and on earth and under the earth, and every tongue confess that Jesus Christ is Lord, to the glory of God the Father' (2:9–11). Here, in magnificent summary, are the Father's approval and vindication of the Son.

When Paul says that God gave Jesus 'the name that is above every name', he is saying much more than that the Father simply 'renames' him or the like. In the ancient world, names were more than convenient labels. What is meant here is that God assigns Jesus a 'name' that reflects what he has achieved and that acknowledges who he is. Probably the 'name' that Paul has in mind is 'Lord' – and inevitably this title brings with it echoes of many Old Testament passages. In Isaiah, God declares, 'I am the LORD; that is my name!' (Is. 42:8). The Hebrew is 'I am YAHWEH': God is the Eternal One, the God who discloses himself through his covenantal name (*cf.* Exod. 3:14). But when that Hebrew word was rendered in Greek, it was commonly translated simply 'Lord' (*Kyrios*). Jesus has achieved this same 'lordship', this same status with his Father, over the whole broken universe – not because there was no sense in which he had it before, but because there is a sense in which he now achieves it, for the first time, as the God-man, as the crucified and risen Redeemer. That the New Testament should quote Isaiah 42 on this matter is particularly significant, for the context shows that this honour belongs to God alone: 'I am the LORD; that is my name! *I will not give my glory to another or my praise to idols*' (Is. 42:8). To give such a title to Jesus, therefore, is tantamount to confessing Jesus' deity, but now as the triumphant, once-crucified and now reigning, resurrected God-man.

One cannot help but be reminded of Jesus' teaching in the gospel of John: the Father has determined that all should honour the Son even as they honour the Father (John 5:23). Every knee in heaven and on earth and under the earth shall bow *to him*. Here, too, the language is drawn from Isaiah, and once again the context of the passage is presupposed. In Isaiah 45 God declares:

Turn to me and be saved,
　all you ends of the earth;
　for I am God, and there is no other.
By myself I have sworn,
　my mouth has uttered in all integrity
　a word that will not be revoked:
Before me every knee will bow;
　by me every tongue will swear.
They will say of me, 'In the LORD alone
　are righteousness and strength.'
All who have raged against him will come to him and be
　put to shame.
But in the LORD all the descendants of Israel
　will be found righteous and will exult. (Is. 45:22–25)

Once again, the implications for who Jesus is, if such words as these are unhesitatingly applied to him, are staggering. To confess that Jesus Christ is Lord, using the language of this passage in Isaiah ('Before me every knee will bow'), is a transparent ascription of deity to Jesus Christ. Yet even so, Jesus is distinguished from God the Father: it is *God* who has exalted Jesus to the highest place. Moreover, the confession that 'Jesus Christ is Lord' is 'to the glory of God the Father' (2:10, 11). Some of the rudiments of what would later be called the doctrine of the Trinity are coming together in a passage like this.

Not for a moment can this passage be used to support universalism, the view that every single person in the entire world will finally be saved. In the Isaiah 45 passage, everyone confesses that in the LORD alone are righteousness and strength; everyone bows the knee. Nevertheless, 'All who have raged against him will come to him and be put to shame' (45:24). So here in Philippians 2 every tongue will confess that Jesus Christ is Lord, but it does not follow that every tongue will confess Jesus Christ as Lord out of happy submission. The text promises that Jesus has the last word, that he is utterly vindicated, that in the end no opposition against him will stand. There will not be universal salvation; there will be universal confession as to who he is.

That means that either we repent and confess him by faith as Lord now, or we will confess him in shame and terror on the last day. But confess him we will.

Perhaps you have talked to someone about the Lord Jesus, only to be rebutted in the following terms: 'Look, I'm pleased if you think this Jesus helps you. If he makes you feel better and enables you to cope and find some sort of significance in life, I'm happy for you. But frankly, I don't need your religion. I like you as a friend, but if this friendship is going anywhere, not to put to fine a point on it, you and this Jesus will have to keep off my back.'

What do you say?

One of the things you must say, sooner or later, and only in the kindest possible way, is something like this: 'You *are* a friend, and I wouldn't want to lose your friendship. But I have to insist that the Jesus I talk about is not some sort of personalized therapy. The Jesus I am talking about made you. You owe him. And one day you will have to give an account of your life to him. Every knee will bow to him sooner or later, whether in joy or in shame and fear. Not to see this is already a mark of horrible lostness from which only he can enable you to escape.'

In other words, the claim that is being made is not of a Jesus who is domesticated, easily marginalized, psychologically privatized, remarkably sanitized, merely personal. He is one with God, yet he died on the cross to redeem us to himself. Elsewhere Paul insists that all things were made by him and for him (Col. 1:16). Now he insists that the Father has vindicated him in his humiliation and sacrifice, and every knee will bow before him.

This is a wonderful passage. Unqualified divine majesty unites with the immeasurable divine self-sacrifice. And now, Paul insists, 'Your attitude should be the same as that of Christ Jesus' (2:5).

Indeed, that is what the surrounding paragraphs tease out. We may summarize their arguments in the following three points:

We are called not only to believe on Christ but also to suffer for him (1:27–30)

We must begin by recognizing how important conduct is for the apostle. *'Whatever happens'*, Paul writes, 'conduct yourselves in a manner worthy of the gospel of Christ' (1:27). The words 'Whatever happens' are the NIV's attempt to render the thought in the Greek's peculiar expression, 'Only this' or 'This one thing': the idea is that whatever else may be mandated, whatever pressures may be brought to bear, 'whatever happens', certain things are central – and they focus on conduct.

The initial description of the conduct is staggering: 'conduct yourselves *in a manner worthy of the gospel of Christ'*. Clearly the standard is immensely high. But what exactly do these words mean?

Certainly they are not suggesting that we ourselves become worthy of the gospel, as if Christ sets up a standard and then somehow by dint of effort we become worthy of it and gain its benefit. The gospel is the good news that Christ died and rose again for sinners. By the death and resurrection of his Son, by the power of the Spirit whom he has sent, God has transferred us out of the kingdom of darkness and into the kingdom of the Son he loves (Col. 1:13). Already we have received the Spirit as the down-payment of the promised inheritance, and one day we shall enjoy the inestimable glories of the new heaven and the new earth. To conduct ourselves 'in a manner worthy of the gospel of Christ' therefore does not suggest we should try harder in order to secure something, but argues that because something has already been secured for us we should try harder out of gratitude and out of frank recognition that this is what the gospel has saved us for. We are to be diligent to live up to the good news that we have received, the good news that has saved us.

The verb 'conduct yourselves' was sometimes used in the ancient world to refer to conduct becoming faithful citizens. The Greeks were to 'conduct themselves as citizens' in such and such a fashion. There may be some corporate overtones in these words when they are applied to the conduct of believers in the church, in this citizenship of the kingdom.

But we must primarily ask, 'What conduct does Paul have in mind that is worthy of the gospel?' The next lines flesh out what is expected. The kind of conduct that Paul wants is the consistent kind that acts the same way whether an apostle is looking over your shoulder or not: 'whether I come and see you or only hear about you in my absence', Paul writes (1:27). The conduct that he wants to discover consistently displayed in them is that they 'stand firm in one spirit, contending as one man for the faith of the gospel without being frightened in any way' by those who oppose them (1:27–28). This unity, this standing firm in one spirit, this 'contending as one man for the faith of the gospel', serves as a double sign: 'This is a sign to them that they will be destroyed, but that you will be saved – and that by God' (1:28). In other words, your change in character, your united stand in defence of the gospel, your ability to withstand with meekness and without fear the opposition that you must endure, constitute a sign. That sign speaks volumes, both to the outside world and to the Christian community. It is a sign of judgment against the world that is mounting the opposition; it is a sign of assurance that these believers really are the people of God and will be saved on the last day.

So conduct worthy of the gospel is in the first instance a corporate unity and steadfastness in defence of the gospel that cheerfully, meekly, and without fear withstands all opposition and boldly promotes the gospel. To put it bluntly, conduct worthy of the gospel is above all conduct that promotes the gospel. What could be more appropriate? The most appropriate way to live, in response to the glorious good news that has saved and transformed you, is to behave in such a way, with other believers, that you actively contend for the faith. Such conduct will prove to be a sign of assurance for you, and a sign of impending judgment to those who will not hear.

Paul then adds a few lines that identify an intrinsic connection between this conduct and the gospel of the cross for which they are to contend. Paul tells the Philippians, 'For it has been granted to you on behalf of Christ not only to believe on him, but also to suffer for him' (1:29). Their call to suffer on behalf of the gospel has been *granted* to them: it is a gracious gift from God! Not only have they enjoyed the privilege of coming to faith, they currently enjoy the privilege of suffering for Christ – 'not only to believe on him', Paul writes, 'but also to suffer for him'.

That is not the way we normally think of suffering, not even the suffering of persecution. But it is what Paul says. *If their salvation has been secured by the suffering of another on their behalf, their discipleship is to be demonstrated in their own suffering on his behalf.*

Of course, our suffering for Christ is not *exactly* the same as Christ's suffering for us. His suffering is the suffering of the God-man, the suffering of the one who enjoyed equality with God, the suffering that secured the forgiveness of others, the suffering of a guiltless victim. Our suffering for Christ cannot add to the atoning significance of his suffering.

Nevertheless, we are called to suffer like him, and for him. Do you recall what Jesus tells his disciples in Mark 8? 'If anyone would come after me, he must deny himself and *take up his cross* and follow me' (Mark 8:34). This language, too, is shocking. To first-century ears, it does not mean that we must all learn to put up with a wart or a disappointment or an obstreperous mother-in-law or an impending mathematics exam: 'We all have our crosses to bear!' No, to first-century ears this means you must take the cross-member on your beaten shoulders, and stagger to the place of crucifixion, and there be executed in blistering agony and shame. To take up your cross means you have passed all point of possible reprieve, all point of hope that you will once again be able to pursue your own interests: you are on your way to death, a dishonourable death at that. So for Jesus' disciples to take up their cross, even to take up their cross *daily* (Luke 9:23), is to say, in spectacularly meta-phorical terms, that they are to come to an end of themselves, no matter how costly that death, in order to follow Jesus.

This lies at the heart of all Christian discipleship. Every time and every place that we refuse to acknowledge this is so, we sin against Christ and need to confess the sin and return to basics. We are to take up our cross daily.

In many parts of the world, this stance includes a willingness to endure overt persecution for Jesus' sake. That is what the Philippians were called to face. In this they were simply following apostolic example: Paul gently reminds them, 'You are going through the same struggle you saw I had, and now hear that I still have' (1:30). Indeed, when the original apostolic band faced their first beating, they left the court 'rejoicing because they had been counted worthy of suffering disgrace for the Name' (Acts 5:41). Doubtless many of us in the West have been relatively cocooned from such outright opposition. But that is not the way it is in many parts of the world.

Missiologists who plot these things tell us that the greatest period of gospel expansion has been the last century and a half. That same century and a half has witnessed more Christian martyrs than the previous eighteen hundred years combined. And it is not at all impossible, if present trends continue in the West, that opposition to the gospel will extend beyond family disapproval, trouble at work, condescension from intellectual colleagues and the like, to concrete persecution.

But learning to take up our cross daily, learning to suffer cheerfully for Jesus' sake, certainly extends beyond physical persecution. One does not have to be a Christian very long before one discovers that there are countless occasions when we are called to put aside self-interest for the sake of Christ. *And in large measure it is the example of Christ and his sufferings that will empower us to tread this path.*

Several years ago I was asked to interview for a video-taping Dr Carl F. H. Henry and Dr Kenneth S. Kantzer. These two American theologians have been at the heart of not a little of the evangelical renaissance in the Western world, especially but not exclusively in America. Each was about eighty years of age at the time of the video-taping. One has written many books; the other brought to birth and nurtured one of the most influential seminaries in the Western world. They have both been connected with Billy Graham, the Lausanne movement, the assorted Congresses on Evangelism, the influential journal *Christianity Today*, and much more. The influence of these Christian leaders extends to the countless numbers of younger pastors and scholars whom they helped to shape, not only by their publications and public teaching but by the personal encouragement at which both excelled. Both men gave lectures for the video cameras before several hundred theological students, and then I interviewed them. Toward the end of that discussion, I asked them a question more or less in these terms: 'You two men have been extraordinarily influential for well-nigh half a century. Without wanting to indulge in cheap flattery, I must say that what is attractive about your ministries is that you have retained integrity. Both of you are strong, yet neither of you is egotistical. You have not succumbed to eccentricity in doctrine, or to individualistic empire-building. In God's good grace, what has been instrumental in preserving you in these areas?'

Both spluttered in deep embarrassment. And then one of them ventured, with a kind of gentle outrage, 'How on earth can anyone be arrogant when standing beside the cross?'

That was a great moment, not least because it was so spontaneous. These men had retained their integrity precisely because they knew their attitude should be the same as that of Jesus Christ (2:5). They knew they had been called not only to believe in Christ but also to suffer for him. If their Master had viewed equality with God not as something he would exploit for personal advantage but as the basis for the humiliating path to the cross, how could they view influential posts of Christian leadership as something they should exploit for personal advantage?

We are called not only to believe on Christ but also to suffer for him.

We are called not only to enjoy the comforts of the gospel but also to pass them on (2:1–11)

That is the burden of the opening lines of chapter 2. One cannot fail to observe that Paul's argument is quite overtly an appeal to experience. The argument, in brief, is this. If you have experienced a number of important and delightful Christian blessings, then there is an entailment: you must act in such and such a manner. To put it another way, Paul argues that if they have enjoyed a certain wealth of experience, then this precious treasure becomes a mandate to specific conduct.

What, then, is this experience to which the apostle makes appeal? And what conduct does he expect?

The appeal to experience is bound up with a series of 'If . . .' clauses in 2:1: 'If you have any encouragement from being united with Christ, if any comfort from his love, if any fellowship with the Spirit, if any tenderness and compassion . . .' In other words, if being Christians has brought them any encouragement, any comfort in times of pain or loneliness as they have basked in the assurance that they are loved by God himself and loved by other believers, if any sense of fellowship or partnership arising from the Spirit's common work in the family of God, if any fresh experience of tenderness and compassion, *then* (verse 2), 'make my joy complete by being like-minded, having the same love, being one in spirit and purpose'.

In other words, Paul asks us if there have been times in our lives when as believers we have sensed God close to us; when we've been aware of his love in tremendous, scarcely describable ways; when we have revelled in the sense of belonging to the fellowship of God's people; when we've received wonderful encouragement as a 'benefit' of the fact that we are Christians. This is, quite bluntly, an appeal to experience. But if these facets of normal Christian living have been part of your experience, you must recognize that a great deal of that experience has come about because other Christians have mediated God's grace to you. They have loved you, cherished you, encouraged you, made you feel part of the partnership of the redeemed. What this means for *you* as a Christian is that you owe the same to others. And if you recognize this point and live by it you will excite the apostle's joy: '. . . then [he writes] make my joy complete by being like-minded [*i.e.* adopting the same stance as those who have ministered to you], having the same love [*i.e.* as that shown to you], being one in spirit and purpose [*i.e.* the entire church is to reflect this same precious, Christ-honouring, God-fearing, self-denying, other-edifying stance]'. And in case this is not cast in terms that are sufficiently practical, Paul spells his point out: 'Do nothing out of selfish ambition or vain conceit, but in humility consider others better than yourselves. Each of you should look not only to your own interests, but also to the interests of others' (2:3–4).

What is this if it is not a principled taking up of one's cross, dying to self-interest for the sake of others?

It takes more grace than I can tell
To play the second fiddle well.

That is what Paul is saying. Others have ministered to you, not least because, as Christians, for Christ's sake and out of care for you they chose to play second fiddle. Now it is your turn. 'Selfish ambition' and 'vain conceit' must go. Self-denying interest in the welfare of others must be our watchword.

For Paul, the issue is finally one of attitude. And the person who has perfectly manifested exactly the right attitude is the Lord Jesus Christ: 'Your attitude should be the same as that of Christ Jesus . . .' (2:5) – whose example is then set forth in the bold lines of the verses that follow (2:6–11).

The point Paul is making, then, is that we have been called not only to enjoy the comforts of the gospel but also to pass them on. If you have received personal benefit from the gospel at the hands of other believers, then maintain the tradition: treat others in such a way that they receive them too. After all, we profess to trust and follow one whose entire mission was characterized by self-denial: in obedience to his heavenly Father he gave and gave and gave.

Your attitude, writes Paul, should be the same as his: give and give and give.

Do we not say as much to our young people sometimes? They go through self-conscious phases in which they think that everyone is staring at them, and that no-one likes them. If they fall into a pattern of self-pity in this regard, sooner or later we say to them, 'Look, stop your whining. To whom have you shown yourself a friend? Those who would have friends must show themselves friendly. Have you looked around your classroom and found the students who are loneliest, most commonly rejected, alone – and tried to befriend them? Why not? Why do you think everyone should be friendly to you when you make no effort to befriend others?'

Of course, all such arguments, as useful as they are, are narrowly pragmatic. Paul's argument is far stronger. *We* owe love and encouragement to others because we *have* received so much; above all, we owe this kind of character and stance to others because we profess to follow Christ Jesus, and that, supremely, is *his* character and stance. It is always deeply disturbing to find some professed Christians, members of the church, who think only of what they get. What a pathetically Christ-denying attitude! Give and give and give. We are called not only to enjoy the comforts of the gospel but also to pass them on.

We are called not only to early steps of faith and obedience, but to an entire life of working out our salvation (2:12–18)

Note how these verses begin: 'Therefore, my dear friends . . .' (2:12). In other words, Paul is now drawing logical connections from the hymn of praise he has just offered up to Christ. There are at least two logical links in the connections he draws. First, 'every knee should bow' (2:10): *therefore* we do well to live in the light of the fact that we shall all bow before Christ on the last day and give an account to him. But more importantly, Christ Jesus, after terrible suffering, was finally vindicated. So shall we be. He obeyed and endured to the end, and was finally vindicated. 'Therefore . . . continue to work out your salvation with fear and trembling' (2:12).

It is vitally important to grasp the connection between God's sovereignty and our responsibility in verses 12 and 13. The text does not say, 'Work to acquire your salvation, for God has done his bit and now it is all up to you.' Nor does it say, 'You may already have your salvation, but now perseverance in it depends entirely on you.' Still less does it say, 'Let go and let God. Just relax. The Spirit will carry you.' Rather, Paul tells us to work out our salvation with fear and trembling, *precisely because* it is God working in us 'both to will and to act according to his good purpose' (2:12–13). Nor is God working merely to strengthen us in *our* willing and acting. Paul's language is stronger than that. God himself is working in us both to will and to act: he works in us at the level of our wills and at the level of our doing. But far from this being a *dis*incentive to press on, Paul insists that this is an incentive. Assured as we are that God works in this way in his people, we should be all the more strongly resolved to will and to act in ways that please our Master.

For reasons too complex to probe here, a great deal of Western thought has gone wrong at precisely this point. We have expended huge quantities of energy pitting God's sovereignty against human responsibility, when the Bible insists that these things belong together. That is true, for example, with respect to election. Many untutored Christians think that any notion of election must be a *dis*incentive to evangelism. Not so for Paul, according to Luke: at one of the apostle's discouraging periods of life and ministry, God encourages him by assuring him that he is to preach on and endure precisely because God already 'has' many people in the city of Corinth, and thus they are bound to be called forth at the right time by the preaching of the Word (Acts 18:9–10).

So also here: God's continuous, gracious, sovereign work in our lives becomes for us an incentive to press on with fear and trembling. And once again, Paul will not let us escape with a merely theoretical point. As in 2:1–4, where he moves from the general exhortation to the specific shape of the command, so he moves here from the general exhortation (2:12–13) to concrete content. If we want to know just what that concrete content is, just what Paul means when he tells us to work out our salvation with fear and trembling, we shall be left in no doubt. He makes three brief points.

(1) 'Do everything without complaining or arguing', Paul writes, 'so that you may become blameless and pure, children of God without fault in a crooked and depraved generation, in which you shine like stars in the universe as you hold out the word of life' (2:14–16a). In other words, Christian contentment, a theme that the apostle takes up later in this epistle, stands out in a selfish, whining, self-pitying world. As Christians 'hold out the word of life', there must not be a trace of self-pity, but a life characterized by sincere gratitude and godly praise.

(2) Moreover, this kind of perseverance is undertaken, at least in part, so as to delight Christian leaders: this, too, is a theme that is about to be developed further, in that the next chapter and a half focus on the importance of emulating the right kind of Christian leaders. So Paul says here that the way the Philippian leaders live, with cheerful godliness as they hold out the word of life, is a commitment undertaken 'in order that I may boast on the day of Christ that I did not run or labour for nothing' (2:16b).

(3) Finally, such Christian perseverance is a form of Christian sacrifice that makes the leaders' sacrifice a complementary capstone to theirs. The argument is subtle, but it is very important.

Paul writes, 'But even if I am being poured out like a drink offering on the sacrifice and service coming from your faith, I am glad and rejoice with all of you' (2:17). In this metaphor, the actions of the Philippians constitute the primary 'sacrifice'. They give themselves to Christ, and commit themselves to pleasing him, whatever the cost. Then, if Paul has to give up his life, his sacrifice is merely a kind of libation poured out on top of their sacrifice. Such a libation is meaningless unless it is poured out on a more substantial sacrifice. But their Christian living is that sacrifice; Paul's martyrdom, should it occur, or the pains and sufferings and persecutions he faces as an apostle, are the complementary drink offering poured over theirs. Paul says, in effect, 'If I suffer, or even lose my life, in a sacrifice poured out on top of your principled self-denial, I am *delighted*. What I do not want is to die a martyr's death without any corresponding fruit in your life. As it is, whatever small sacrifice I am called upon to make is but a complementary capstone to the sacrifice that all Christians are called to make. In this I will rejoice. So you too should rejoice and be glad with me' (*cf.* 2:18).

So we are called not only to early steps of faith and obedience, but to an entire life of working out our salvation. This will be characterized by self-denying contentment; by a conscious effort to please mature Christian leaders; and by a cheerful sacrifice that ratifies and endorses the work that more mature Christian leaders have poured into our lives. And all of this is nothing more than learning the entailments of following a crucified Messiah.

In short, we must adopt Jesus' death as a test of our outlook.

One of the great Christian poets of the twentieth century was Amy Carmichael, one of whose compositions captures many themes in this chapter:

From prayer that asks that I may be
Sheltered from winds that beat on Thee,
From fearing when I should aspire,
From faltering when I should climb higher,
From silken self, O Captain, free
The soldier who would follow Thee.

From subtle love of softening things,
From easy choices, weakenings
(Not thus are spirits fortified,
Not this way went the Crucified),
From all that dims Thy Calvary,
O Lamb of God, deliver me.

Give me the love that leads the way,
The faith that nothing can dismay,
The hope no disappointments tire,
The passion that will burn like fire.
Let me not sink to be a clod:
Make me Thy fuel, Flame of God.

Adopt Jesus' death as a test of your outlook.

3

Emulate worthy Christian leaders

Philippians 2:19–3:21

When I was an undergraduate at McGill University in the 1960s,
reading chemistry and mathematics, another Christian student
and I began an evangelistic Bible study in my room in the men's
dorm where we were living. We were both a little nervous, and
didn't want to be outnumbered. So we invited only three unbelievers, expecting that not more than one or two would show up. It
was rather distressing when all three put in an appearance. I had
never done anything like this before. Within a few weeks, sixteen
students squeezed into my little room, and still only two of us
were believers. Doubtless some Christian observers thought it was
going exceedingly well; as for me, I was exceedingly frightened.
The Bible study engendered all kinds of private discussions, and I
soon discovered I was out of my depth.

Mercifully, there was a chap on campus called Dave, a rather
brusque graduate student who was known to be wonderfully
effective in talking to students about his faith and about elementary

biblical Christianity. I was not the only one who on occasion brought our friends and contacts for a little chat with Dave.

On the particular occasion I have in mind, I brought two of the undergraduates from the Bible study down the mountain to Dave's rooms. He was pressed for time, and, as usual, a bit abrupt, but he offered us coffee and promptly turned to the first student.

'Why have you come to see me?' he asked.

The student replied along these lines: 'Well, you know, I've been going to this Bible study and I realize I should probably learn a bit more about Christianity. I'd also like to learn something of Buddhism, Islam, and other world religions. I'm sure I should broaden my perspectives, and this period while I am a university student seems like a good time to explore religion a little. If you can help me with some of it, I'd be grateful.'

Dave stared at him for a few seconds, and then said, 'I'm sorry, I don't have time for you.'

I just about dropped my jaw. The student thus addressed was equally nonplussed, and blurted out, 'I beg your pardon?'

Dave replied, 'I'm sorry, I don't mean to be rude, but I only have so much time. I'm a graduate student with a heavy programme myself. If you have a dilettante's interest in Christianity, I'm sure there are people around who could spend a lot of time and energy showing you the ropes. I can introduce you to some of them, and give you some books. When you're really interested in Christ, come and see me again. But under the present circumstances, I don't have time.'

He turned to the second student. 'Why did you come?'

After listening in on the rebuff administered to the first student, the second may have been a bit cowed. But gamely he ploughed on. 'I come from what you people would call a liberal home. We don't believe the way you do. But it's a good home, a happy home. My parents loved their children, disciplined us, set a good example, and encouraged us to be courteous, honourable, and hard-working. And for the life of me I can't see that you people who think of yourselves as Christians are any better. Apart from a whole lot of abstract theology, what have you got that I haven't?'

This time I held my breath to see what Dave would say. Once again he stared at his interlocutor for a few seconds, and then he simply said, 'Watch me.'

I suppose my mouth dropped open again. The student, whose name was Rick, said something like, 'I'm sorry, I don't understand.'

Dave answered, 'Watch me. Come and live with me for a month, if you like. Be my guest. Watch what I do when I get up, what I do when I'm on my own, how I work, how I use my time, how I talk with people, what my values are. Come with me wherever I go. And at the end of the month, you tell me if there is any difference.'

Rick did not take Dave up on his invitation, at least not in exactly those terms. But he did get to know Dave better, and in due course Rick became a Christian, married a Christian woman, and the two of them, by this time medical doctors, practised medicine and lived their faith both in Canada and overseas.

'Watch me.' At the time I worried about the sheer arrogance that such an invitation seemed to capture. At the same time, my mind recalled the words of the apostle Paul: 'Follow my example, as I follow the example of Christ' (1 Cor. 11:1).[5] Sober observation and reflection assure us that much Christian character is as much caught as taught – that is, it is picked up by constant association with mature Christians.

The general importance of learning by a kind of existential mimicry is well established at every level. Why do Canadian children grow up speaking with Canadian accents? Why is it that if you are reared in Yorkshire you sound like a Yorkshireman, and if you grow up in Dallas you sound like a Texan? We all know the answer: people grow up imitating those around them. For exactly the same reason, parents are concerned that their children have the right kind of friends, because they know that children copy children. If all their friends are violent or vulgar or uncouth, the odds are much greater that their own children will be violent or vulgar or uncouth. This is no less true in the teen years. At that point, the unconscious habit of copying Mummy and Daddy weakens. And yet, thinking themselves to be wonderfully independent, all these teenagers become terribly eager to copy their peers. But they are still imitating *someone*.

Even television operates in this way. It provides a kind of vicarious friendship. In some ways, it might be judged better than a friend: it never talks back – or if, with the advent of interactive television, it does talk back, you can always switch it off. But if you watch thousands of violent deaths before the age of eighteen, it is bound to affect your personality. If you watch sexual promiscuity day in and day out, then even if at one level of your mind you conclude that promiscuity is immoral, in fact your tolerance levels have been subtly altered. You are no longer shocked. And for many people, television provides a sort of moral 'bottom line': they have no other dominating reference point. Multiply such influence by the millions of people who watch, and the effect in society is inevitable: massive moral decline. That is why some wise parents, if they have a TV at all, limit how much they and their children watch, and when they permit their children to watch they insist that one parent or the other be present, not least so that the content can be talked about and evaluated afterward.

But mimicry is not restricted to the secular arena. It is no less important in our Christian pilgrimage. How did you learn to pray? If you were reared in a Christian home, doubtless you learned to pray by hearing your parents pray. Perhaps, too, they taught you some very simple prayers to be prayed at bedtime: 'Now I lay me down to sleep . . .' or 'Gentle Jesus, meek and mild. . . .' If you spring from a very conservative Christian home, where the Authorized Version exposed you to archaic English, your first public prayer, perhaps when you were six or eight years old, probably sounded like this: 'We thank Thee, blessed God, that in Thy mercy Thou hast vouchsafed to us Thy grace through the merits of Thy Son and our Saviour, Jesus Christ.' But if you were not converted until your third year at university, in a UCCF or Navigators or Campus Crusade group, and you spring from a home that never brought you to church at all, your first public prayer probably sounded something like this: 'We just wanna thank you, Jesus, for being here.' In *both* cases you learned to pray by listening to others.

Modelling, modelling: it takes place all the time, whether we take it into account or not. This is true even of adults. Of course, we enjoy a wider range of choices of people after whom we want to pattern our lives, but the modelling goes on. That is why advertising works. Companies spend billions of pounds a year selling toothpaste or a car or a stereo system visually linked to some beautiful blonde or some amazing hunk. The companies would not do this if they did not think it worked. We may not be so naïve as to think, 'If only I used that toothpaste, I would look like that, too!' Yet at some deep level, advertisements must work for most of us, or companies would not pay their billions to produce them.

Some of our habits of imitation are frankly amusing. When I was still a young preacher, and still single, my mother, who was my best critic until my wife came along, one day asked me, after a sermon, where I had picked up my grotesque leer. I assured her I did not have a clue what she was talking about. She told me that sometimes in full flow I would pause, lean over the pulpit, drop my bottom lip, and leer. Once I thought about it, I realized where I had picked the habit up. Another minister, who had befriended me, taken me aside weekly and taught me the rudiments of intercessory prayer, had the same habit. I revered that man, and on him the facial contortion looked, in my eyes at least, thoughtful and reflective. Probably he was entirely unaware of his mannerism. But sure enough, I had picked it up, and on me it came across as nothing but leering at the congregation.

How, then, shall new Christians learn to talk Christianly, think Christianly, evaluate society Christianly, live in families Christianly, learn to witness, learn to give, learn to develop godly habits of life? Of course, much is said on all these topics in Scripture: many believers will find their lives shaped simply by reading and re-reading Scripture. Nor would I want to minimize the powerful, inner work of the Holy Spirit. But the Spirit most commonly uses means. And those means include the modelling that more experienced Christians offer.

Perhaps I should pause and comment on one element of this challenge, an element that affects what I do every week. There was a time when the majority of those who came to our seminaries and theological colleges to offer themselves for the ministry sprang from Christian homes. Many of them were themselves children of the manse or of the mission field. This is today decreasingly the case. Our students come from all sorts of colourful backgrounds. Many were converted only in their twenties. Most were never inculturated in a particular ecclesiastical heritage; some of them come from broken homes, and not a few of them once took drugs. How on earth can we be expected to prepare them for pastoral ministry, if we restrict ourselves to whatever we can put into their lives in the classroom? Oh, they are genuinely Christians, all right – but many of them are carrying so much emotional baggage, and they are so inexperienced in mature ecclesiastical cultures, that three years in a seminary classroom are not going to resolve all the issues. Seminaries and theological colleges can do some things extremely well. But they must not be seen as pastors' finishing schools: a great deal of the polish must be administered *within the context of the local church*. In that context pastoral apprentices learn much more of living, ministering, preaching, interacting graciously with obstreperous people, bearing one another's burdens, praying fervently, weeping with those who weep and laughing with those who laugh, *by observing how mature Christians excel in all of these areas.*

So the question is not *whether* we shall learn from others by conscious and unconscious mimicry, but *what* we shall learn, and *from whom* we shall learn it. And that question is massively addressed in the passage before us. It is implicit throughout the passage, and it becomes explicit at discrete points: *e.g.* 3:17, 'Join with others in following my example, brothers, and take note of those who live according to the pattern we gave you.' A verse like this is not narrowly doctrinal: it is existential, it concerns how you live. Similarly, part of the reason Paul describes Timothy and Epaphroditus at the end of chapter 2, and is so self-revealing about his own motives and habits in chapter 3, is that he is concerned to establish and reinforce good models. He is not stooping to cheap flattery of his colleagues, nor is he indulging in self-congratulation. His aim is to provide clear Christian examples that younger and less experienced Christians ought to emulate. For if they do not have such models, or if they are not encouraged to follow them, they are likely to follow poor or misleading or even dangerous examples.

So whom should we follow? Which Christians should be our models?

Emulate those who are interested in the well-being of others, not their own (2:19–21)

Paul's opening words regarding Timothy constitute a wonderful accolade: 'I hope in the Lord Jesus to send Timothy to you soon, that I also may be cheered when I receive news about you. I have no-one else like him, who takes a genuine interest in your welfare' (2:19–20). One of the reasons Paul is sending Timothy is that when Timothy returns Paul will find out how the Philippians are getting on (2:19). But the other reason is that Timothy himself reflects Paul's attitude exactly: he 'takes a genuine interest in your welfare' (2:20). When Paul says, 'I have no-one else like him', he probably does not mean that he knows no other Christians anywhere who exhibit the same kind of maturity, but that of the helpers he has with him at the moment Timothy is outstanding: none of the others can touch him in this particular, the transparent interest Timothy takes in the well-being of others.

There are many different styles of leadership. Some leaders live to be admired, to be praised. Without ever being so crass as to say so, they give the impression that the church exists and flourishes primarily because of their gifts, and the least the church can do in return is offer constant adulation. But that is not Timothy's attitude. He lives for them; he is genuinely interested in their well-being.

Of course, in the light of the letter so far, this is nothing other than a sign that Timothy follows not only Paul but Jesus. Although Christ Jesus enjoyed equality with God, he did not think of such equality as something to be exploited, but adopted the form of a servant. He became a human being, a man, and then obediently went to his odious death on the cross. Those who follow Jesus Christ inevitably learn to cast self-interest and self-comfort and self-focus to one side. Paul knows that as a general rule 'everyone looks out for his own interests, not those of Jesus Christ' (2:21). But Timothy has eclipsed that narrow snare.

So whom will you follow? Which contemporary Christians will serve you well as good models? Emulate those who are interested in the well-being of others, not their own. Be on the alert for Christians who really do exemplify this basic Christian attitude, this habit of helpfulness. They are never the sort who strut their way into leadership with inflated estimates of their own importance. They are the kind who cheerfully pick up after other people. They are not offended if no-one asks after them; they are too busy asking after others. They are the kind who are constantly seeking to do good spiritually, to do good materially, to do good emotionally. They are committed to the well-being of others. Watch them. Watch how they act, how they talk, how they react. Talk with them; learn their heartbeat. Imitate them. Emulate those who are interested in the well-being of others, not their own.

Emulate those who have proved themselves in hardship (2:22–30)

Paul reminds the Philippians that they 'know that Timothy has proved himself, because as a son with his father he has served with me in the work of the gospel' (2:22). The analogy is a lovely one. In the ancient world, before the industrial revolution, most sons ended up doing vocationally what their fathers did. If your father is a farmer, the chances are very high that you will become a farmer; if your father is a baker, most likely you will become a baker. And your primary apprenticeship is to your father: it is your Dad who teaches you the tricks of the trade, who gradually teaches you all he knows, and, step by step, increases your load of knowledgeable responsibility.

The image is less forceful for us today, not only because most of our children will not follow the vocational path followed by their parents, but because most of our children do not really see us at work. In the ancient world, children observed their parents working, and learned the trade by working alongside them. But my children do not accompany me to the seminary where I teach. Only rarely do they accompany me when I go somewhere to preach. They cannot share with me endless hours in the library or in my study; unless it takes place at the dinner table, they cannot listen in on the counsel I am expected to give to many who come to see me. So even if one of my children were to end up in vocational ministry, not much of their training would be grounded in working beside me. And so it is for most of us.

But Paul's analogy is based on the ancient model. Timothy has learned his Christianity and his first steps in Christian ministry from Paul, as a son learns from his father. Timothy has enjoyed Paul as his spiritual father, his mentor. In that context he has been tested: he 'has proved himself', Paul writes. So Paul is entirely at ease about sending him: 'I hope, *therefore*, to send him as soon as I see how things go with me' (2:23). Timothy will serve as a kind of forerunner to Paul, who hopes to come along shortly himself: 'And I am confident in the Lord that I myself will come soon' (2:24).

Then there is Epaphroditus (2:25–30). This paragraph of Scripture shows Paul to be a leader characterized by deep empathy and compassion. Wonderfully tender lines are found in verse 29, where Epaphroditus is held up as a man to be honoured: 'Welcome him in the Lord with great joy, and honour men like him'.

The circumstances are more or less clear. The opening words suggest that Epaphroditus was himself from Philippi. 'I think it is necessary to send *back* to you Epaphroditus, my brother': Epaphroditus had been the messenger of the Philippians to Paul, a messenger 'sent to take care of my needs' (2:25), Paul writes. Epaphroditus had borne their financial gift to the apostle (4:10, 14–18); probably he had also supported Paul by his own hard work once he was on site. But now Paul wants to send him back to Philippi. That is what Epaphroditus wants, too, and Paul recognizes the fact: 'For he longs for all of you and is distressed because you heard he was ill' (2:26). That is a remarkable assessment. Epaphroditus was not distressed because he was ill, but because he knew by now that his Philippian brothers and sisters in Christ had heard he was ill. Epaphroditus was distressed because he feared his fellow believers would be distressed on his account.

However much Paul applauds the attitude of Epaphroditus, he will not let him get away with downplaying the seriousness of the illness. The apostle carefully lays out the gravity of the trauma through which the Philippian emissary has passed: 'Indeed he was ill, and almost died' (2:27). If he survived, it was a singular mercy from God, a mercy not only to Epaphroditus, but also to Paul, who was thus spared a profound sorrow (2:27). Paul can scarcely imagine what he would have done if Epaphroditus had been taken from him. 'Therefore I am all the more eager to send him, so that when you see him again you may be glad and I may have less anxiety' (2:28) – that is, my mind will be relieved if he reaches home safely and you enjoy a happy reunion.

Those, in brief, are the circumstances that lie behind this paragraph. But note how Paul casts the matter. He refers to Epaphroditus in the most collegial manner ('my brother, fellow-worker and fellow-soldier', 2:25), and then concludes *with an exhortation to the Philippians to hold up such leaders as Christians to be honoured and emulated*. 'Welcome him in the Lord with great joy', Paul writes, 'and honour men like him, because he almost died for the work of Christ, risking his life to make up for the help you could not give me' (2:29–30). In short: emulate those who have proved themselves in hardship, not the untested upstart and the self-preening peacock.

One should also ponder Paul's choice of one particular word in this paragraph. Epaphroditus, Paul says, risked his life 'to make up for the *help* you could not give me'. The word here rendered 'help' is a strange one in this context. It is a word that might more commonly be rendered 'religious service' or the like, a word that would be used in the context of discussing worship. But what might Paul be meaning when he says that Epaphroditus risked his life to make up for the 'religious service' that the Philippians themselves could not render?

In recent years, the Western church has produced quite a few books and discussions on the nature of Christian worship. Some want worship to become more liturgical. They are usually the people who do not themselves belong to liturgical traditions. Others want worship to become much less liturgical: they are usually the believers who belong to liturgical traditions. The 'grass on the other side of the fence' syndrome works in this debate as efficiently as in other debates. For some people, worship means pipe organs; for others, it means guitars and synthesizers. For some, it means sonorous hymns written at least a century or two ago, and preferably longer; for others, it is not truly Spirit-driven and fresh unless it is characterized by no musical composition more than twenty years old. When people ask what worship is, charismatics tend to begin with 1 Corinthians 12 and 14, musicians tend to begin with David's choirs, sacramentalists begin with 1 Corinthians 11 and other references to the Lord's Supper, and New Testament specialists tend to begin by trying to identify hymn fragments in the New Testament. For many of us, worship is what you do *before* the sermon, but certainly does not include the sermon itself. Thus we carefully distinguish between the 'worship leader' and the preacher: the worship leader doesn't preach and the preacher doesn't lead in worship. After the sermon, if you sing a little more you have returned to worship. But few have tried to construct a genuinely biblical theology of worship.

An exception is a book by David Peterson,[6] who rightly points out that under the old covenant, worship, along with all the vocabulary associated with it (sacrifice, prayer, adoration, praise, service, priest), is primarily bound up with the tabernacle and then with the temple. But when one turns to the new covenant, the worship terminology is not so narrowly constrained. Worship terminology is not restricted to, say, the Lord's Supper, or to the public meetings of the church. What is remarkable about worship terminology under the new covenant is that it *characteristically touches all of life*. The well-known passage at the beginning of Romans 12 is a case in point: 'Therefore, I urge you, brothers, in view of God's mercy, *to offer* yourselves as *living sacrifices*, holy and pleasing to God – this is your spiritual act of worship' (Rom. 12:1). In the New Testament, all genuine believers constitute a royal priesthood. In Romans 15 worship is bound up with evangelism. Jesus himself taught that worship is no longer bound up with the cultic in one geographical location or another, whether Jerusalem with its temple or the mountains of Gerizim and Ebal in Samaria (John 4). No, the Father seeks those who will worship him in spirit and in truth. Here, as elsewhere, worship embraces all of life and every location. Worship is the consistent offering of all of one's life and time and energy and body and resources to God; it is profound God-centredness. There is a sense in which true Christians should never be *not* worshipping.

So well-instructed Christians must never suggest that they come together to worship, if by this they mean that during the rest of the week they have not been worshipping and now they gather on Sunday morning at 11:00 a.m. primarily to discharge their obligation to worship. For the Christian, worship embraces all of life. But, you reply, does this mean that Christians *do not* or *should not* worship when they come together? That is what some have suggested: Christian corporate meetings are *not* for worship but primarily for instruction. But that, too, misses the point. It is not that we worship all week and refuse to worship when we come together! Rather, when we gather together, we worship corporately, as we have been worshipping individually all week. This corporate worship includes corporate praise, mutual edification, instruction in the Word and Christian truth, celebration of Christ's death in the memorial that he left behind for that purpose. Thus the sermon itself is not *un*-worship; it is part of our corporate worship, both a sign of it and a profound incitement to it.

This is at least part of the structure of New Testament thought about worship. Once this material has been properly absorbed, it may be useful to discuss pipe organs and guitars. But before absorbing what the Bible has to say on the subject of worship, such discussion is likely to be premature.

In the context of these new-covenant emphases on worship, the reason Paul chooses the particular word that he does when he addresses the Philippians becomes reasonably clear. Epaphroditus almost died for the work of Christ, 'risking his life to make up for the *religious service* you could not give me' (2:30). The Philippian believers would very much have wanted to help Paul personally. All such help he viewed as 'religious service' – part and parcel of their God-centred living, their God-centred service, their God-centred offering of themselves as a continuous sacrifice to God. Whether their help was money, or prayers, or moral encouragement, or concrete evangelism, or some other assistance offered to the apostle, Paul saw it as an element of their service, their worship. And if they were too far away to perform such service personally, then they were happy to send an emissary, whose 'religious service', whose 'worship', was at the risk of his very life. There is nothing to suggest that this risk of life and limb was the result of persecution: probably Epaphroditus fell ill because of some very ordinary bug. But on the other hand, he would not have caught the bug if he had remained comfortably at home on the shores of the Aegean. It was his commitment to help Paul and further the gospel that brought him to Rome, a trip that almost cost him his life – and all of this is bound up with 'religious service', worship if you will, that is simultaneously a help to Paul and an offering to God. And very little of what Epaphroditus brought Paul had much to do with Sunday morning at 11:00 a.m.

Such a view of worship is not designed to depreciate what we do corporately on Sunday morning. It is designed, rather, to ensure that all of life is lived in faithful and delighted obedience to the gospel of God, with the result that what we do corporately when we come together on Sunday morning, or any other time, is the overflow of our experience of God, and a place to be refreshed in the joy of the Lord as we think through his Word, express our praise and thanksgiving, and deepen our links of love with him and with one another. But the point to recognize is that under the terms of the new covenant, worship is bound up with all of life. We live holistically under the grace of God. Either we are God-centred in all that we do, or we are not. If we are, then God's words and ways are precious to us, and all of our living is offered in worship; if we are not, we are in rebellion against God, and nothing that we do is true worship.

The reason this excursus is important to my main point is that mature Christian living is inextricably bound up with this attitude of self-sacrificial service offered up to God, not least in the promotion of the gospel and for the good of other believers. Emulate those who have proved themselves in hardship, not the untested upstart and the self-promoting peacock.

I well remember a Christian leader who a number of years ago used to give this advice to younger Christians: 'One of the most important things in Christian leadership', he would solemnly intone, 'is never to admit any weaknesses. If you admit weaknesses, others will exploit them to your detriment.' Astonishing! Surely there are many areas in which Christians *must* acknowledge their weaknesses. Isn't that Paul's policy, when in 2 Corinthians 12 he insists he has learned to 'boast' of his weaknesses so that Christ's strength might be made perfect in him?

Indeed, in the same passage, Paul circumscribes what he says about his own spiritual experiences, precisely because he is fearful that people will think too much of him. If he must be assessed, he wants to be judged by what he says and does in the public arena, not by laying claim to spiritual experiences no-one else can test (2 Cor. 12:5–6). What is remarkable is the way Paul's stance differs from our own. Many Christians today, even Christian leaders, go through life fearful that people will think too little of them. They quickly become irritable if someone, especially a junior, is praised more than they. But Paul goes through life fearful that people will think too much. Follow a leader like that! He has been tested by hardship, and he is not an untested upstart or a self-promoting peacock. Emulate such leaders.

Emulate those whose constant confidence and boast are in Christ Jesus and in nothing else (3:1–9)

Paul begins, according to most of our English versions, with the words 'Finally, my brothers . . .' There have been a lot of jokes levelled at preachers because of that 'Finally'. One child allegedly asked his Dad what the preacher meant when he said 'Finally', and his father muttered in reply, 'Nothing.' Some critics, eager to be sceptical about the Bible, argue that this word proves that this letter was not written at one time by the apostle, but is a pastiche of sources, one of which ended up with this paragraph beginning with 'Finally'. Some clumsy editor slapped the paragraph into this location, and the result is nonsense.

In fact, our common translations have made things unnecessarily difficult for us. The Greek word used here often served, at this late period of Greek, as a loose connective particle, like our 'So then'. What Paul is doing is picking up the theme of rejoicing he introduced in 2:17–18. There he insists that as he is prepared to offer himself as a kind of drink offering poured out on *their* self-sacrifice, he is glad and rejoices with all of them, and he wants them to rejoice with him. In the following verses, he has told of two helpers, Timothy and Epaphroditus, who have similarly displayed this willingness to suffer for the sake of others, a stance which, ironically, brings joy. 'So then, my brothers', Paul now writes (3:1), 'rejoice in the Lord!'

That sounds very much like a transitional comment. In the verses that follow, although Paul will warn against some false teachers in the strongest language, the issues still turn, in part, on this willingness to put aside what the world and self-interest might choose, in order to pursue knowledge of Christ. But from Paul's perspective, this is so wonderful a privilege that what starts off as self-abnegation turns out to be exactly what the thoughtful Christian wants to do anyway, simply because there is nothing better and finer and more enjoyable than knowing Jesus Christ.

Paul has told the Philippians these things before. That is why he now says, 'It is no trouble for me to write the same things to you again, and it is a safeguard for you' (3:1). The 'same things' to which Paul refers are probably not things that Paul has already said in this letter, since there is no really close parallel between these next verses and what Paul has already written in this epistle.

Probably what Paul is referring to is what he has earlier taught them. A little review in spiritual matters is entirely salutary.

So he embarks on this review. 'Watch out for those dogs, those men who do evil, those mutilators of the flesh. For it is we who are the circumcision, we who worship by the Spirit of God, who glory in Christ Jesus, and who put no confidence in the flesh' (3:2–3). This is strong language. Almost certainly Paul is referring to a recurring problem in the churches that he founds. There were many devout Jews who were prepared to believe that Jesus was the promised Messiah, but who thought that for Gentiles to accept this Jewish Messiah they would have to become Jews first. That means they would have to be circumcised and take on responsibility for observing the law of Moses. In other words, they think of Christianity as Judaism plus a little extra, almost as a sect of Judaism.

Paul does not share their view. He insists that they are misreading the Hebrew Bible, what we call the Old Testament. The old-covenant Scriptures do not establish eternal structures of religious observance that are capped by the coming of Jesus. Rather, they anticipate his coming, they look forward to his coming, they announce his coming – but it is his coming that is the ultimate hope. In this view, although the temple in the Old Testament had many functions, one of its most important functions was in pointing to him who would *be* the 'temple', that is, the supreme place of sacrifice and the supreme meeting-place between God and his people (John 2). The priesthood of the old covenant looks forward to the one, supreme high priest 'after the order of Melchizedek' (Heb. 5–7). The sacrifices ultimately anticipate one who would shed his own blood, not the blood of bulls and goats that can never finally take away sin (Heb. 9:11–28). The Passover not only looked back to the blessed night when the angel of death 'passed over' the homes of those who put the blood of the Passover lamb on the two doorposts and on the lintel, but it looks forward to Christ our Passover lamb who was sacrificed for us (1 Cor. 5:7), as Paul himself argued.

For many conservative Jews, the sign of entrance into the covenant was circumcision. That is why circumcision was such a crucial issue for them. If Gentiles had to become Jews before they became Christians, then they had to be circumcised before they became Christians. To put it the other way round: when Jews told Gentile Christians they had to be circumcised before they could be real and proper Christians, they were saying, in effect, that Gentiles could not really enjoy the blessings of the gospel, the blessings of Christ Jesus, until they had undergone the rite of circumcision, and solemnly pledged themselves to live under the ancient Jewish law. But Paul's point is that those who argue in this way do not really understand what the Old Testament Scriptures say about circumcision. Already in the Old Testament, the biblical writers make clear that circumcision of the heart is more important than literal circumcision (*e.g.* Deut. 10:16; 30:6; Jer. 9:25; Ezek. 44:9). Paul agrees, but he goes a step further: under the terms of the new covenant inaugurated by the Lord Jesus, circumcision of the flesh is no longer the sign of entrance into the covenant community. The distinguishing feature of a Christian, of a new covenant believer, is that he or she has undergone 'circumcision of the heart, by the Spirit, not by the written code' (Rom. 2:29).

That is the background to the challenge that Paul faces. Very often after he has preached the gospel in some town or city and then moved on to the next needy place, other Jews have dogged his path and tried to convince his new converts that if they are to view themselves as Christians at all they must submit to circumcision and thus signal that they are prepared to take on the law of Moses. Whether such people have arrived in Philippi and are beginning to trouble the church, or, alternatively, Paul fears that their arrival is impending and dangerous, he takes the opportunity to warn the Philippian Christians about them and thus to arm them with sound information so that they will be able to withstand the assault.

'Watch out for those dogs, those men who do evil, those mutilators of the flesh' (3:2). Paul's point is that although many conservative Jews spoke of themselves as 'the circumcision', and of Gentiles as unclean 'dogs', in reality by rejecting Jesus Christ they are themselves the 'dogs' – and their vaunted circumcision is nothing more than mutilation if it claims prerogatives for itself beyond its proper place in redemptive history. In particular, if it relativizes Christ and fails to see that he is the *fulfilment* of Old Testament types and models, it is positively 'evil'. For in fact 'it is we who are the circumcision' (3:3) – not, of course, the circumcision of the flesh, but that of the changed life and heart brought about by the gospel. It is 'we who worship by the Spirit of God, who glory in Christ Jesus, and who put no confidence in the flesh' (3:3).

Paul is not saying these things out of barely suppressed jealousy, as if he were frustrated because he himself enjoyed none of the privileges of status, training and discipline that were a godly part of the heritage of the old covenant. Far from it: Paul himself, if he were so minded, could cheerfully boast about the many forms of religious 'confidence' that he himself enjoyed. 'If anyone else thinks he has reasons to put confidence in the flesh, I have more' (3:4), Paul writes – and then lists what he has in mind, the kinds of things that would fly very well in some conservative Jewish circles in the first century.

For a start, he himself had been 'done' on the eighth day of his life: he was circumcised, a full-blooded Jew, covenantally belonging to the people of Israel. Not only so, he sprang from the tribe of Benjamin, one of only two tribes that did not rebel against the Davidic dynasty. Culturally, he was a 'Hebrew of the Hebrews':

though born in Tarsus and thoroughly acquainted with Graeco-Roman culture, he was steeped in the language and culture of his racial and religious heritage, receiving his educational formation in Jerusalem. So far as the various Jewish 'sects' or parties were concerned, and their varied stances on how far the law of Moses was to be observed, he was brought up a Pharisee: strict, disciplined, informed, widely respected. Nor was he a Pharisee in name only: he understood the claims of the fledgling Christian community well enough to realize that they could not be ignored, and went after them with persecuting zeal. In fact, as for the full sweep of righteousness under the law (a better rendering of the Greek than NIV's 'legalistic righteousness'), Paul was, quite frankly, 'faultless' (3:6). By this he does not mean he had attained sinless perfection. Far from it: the law provided the remedies for sin, prescribing certain sacrifices, teaching earnest young Jews to look to the God who was addressed each 'day of atonement' by the high priest who sprinkled the blood of animals in the Most Holy Place, to atone both for the his own sins and for the sins of the people. Paul followed the entire pattern of religious life carefully. He was utterly exemplary.

'But whatever was to my profit', Paul writes, 'I now consider loss for the sake of Christ' (3:7). Everything in the credit column has been transferred to the debit column; Christ alone stands in the credit column.

And then, fearing perhaps that his point has still not been made with sufficient force, Paul resorts to even stronger language. 'What is more,' he writes, 'I consider everything a loss compared to the surpassing greatness of knowing Christ Jesus my Lord, for whose sake I have lost all things' (3:8). And lose them he did. He was written off by his erstwhile friends and intellectual peers. He lost the security of a home, becoming a constant traveller with no fixed abode. The kinds of sufferings he endured make for an astonishing list (see 2 Cor. 11:23–29). Yet none of this is uttered by way of complaint. We would be misrepresenting Paul in the worst possible way if we were to conclude that these lines betray an apostle who sometimes indulges in a little pity-party. Regarding the things that were taken away from him, Paul calmly asserts, 'I consider them rubbish, that I may gain Christ and be found in him, not having a righteousness of my own that comes from the law, but that which is through faith in Christ – the righteousness that comes from God and is by faith' (3:9).

Here, then, Paul exposes his fundamental values. On one side stands everything the world has to offer, including the privileged world of learned and disciplined Judaism. On the other stands Jesus Christ, and 'the righteousness that comes from God and is by faith'. Paul insists there is no contest: Jesus and the righteousness from God that Jesus secures are incomparably to be preferred.

We should pause a moment to reflect on why Paul would make this judgment. The word 'righteousness' could equally be rendered 'justification', and often is. Despite the criticisms voiced by some critics, the word regularly means, in Paul's letters, that God on account of the death of his Son declares certain people 'just' or 'righteous'. Paul quickly and allusively makes three points about this 'justification' or 'righteousness'. (1) It 'comes from God': that is, it is God's gift, secured because God sent his own Son to die for sinners. (2) It is 'by faith': that is, it is secured 'through faith in Christ'. The means of receiving it is faith, and the object of that faith is Christ. (3) This 'righteousness' is set over against whatever Paul could achieve by observing the law – as he puts it, 'a righteousness of my own that comes from the law' (3:9). Paul does not think that those under the old covenant were not really obligated to abide by its stipulations, or that no-one in those days could be right before God. Rather, now that Christ Jesus has come, in fulfilment of the law, he sees the legal requirements of the law in a new way. He holds that even under the old covenant men and women were saved by God's grace, appropriated through faith – but that such faith manifested itself, under the old covenant, in terms of obedience to that covenant. Paul is not depreciating obedience. He is insisting that many Jews, including himself in his pre-Christian days, had come to think of the law in a way that was never intended. Instead of seeing the law as one of the preparations for the righteousness from God that would be secured by the coming and death of the Messiah, the law had increasingly become the basis for being 'righteous' before God. That is why some people, as we have seen, urged that Gentiles had to commit themselves to keeping the whole law, symbolized by submitting themselves to circumcision, before they could properly become Christians (see on 3:2–3, above). Paul will not have it: as far as he is concerned, everything else is rubbish in comparison with gaining Christ, with receiving this righteousness from God that is by faith.

Paul understands that justification is God's word – secured by Christ's death and appropriated by faith. God looks at me through the death of his Son and he declares me just. Paul recognizes that in God's universe, the most important thing is to know God. In a flow of history that inevitably runs toward the judgment, the great judgment in which only God's verdict matters, to be declared righteous by this Creator God, this Judge, is infinitely more precious than anything else one can imagine. It is infinitely more important than having all the laurels – ecclesiastical, academic, societal, financial, personal – in the world. Since that righteousness from God turns absolutely, at this point in redemptive history, on gaining Christ and being found in him (3:8–9), that is what Paul wants above all things. Everything else is just rubbish.

In the flow of the chapter, then, Paul makes these points, at least in part, to insist that the Philippian believers emulate those whose constant confidence and boast are in Christ Jesus, and in nothing else. Most who read these pages, I suspect, will not be greatly tempted to boast about their Jewish ancestry and ancient rights of race and religious heritage. But we may be tempted to brag about still less important things: our wealth, our status, our education, our emotional stability, our families, our political or industrial successes, our denominational alignments – or even over which version of the Bible we use. Be careful of people like that. They tend to see everyone else but those in their little group as somehow inferior. Somewhere along the way they inadvertently – or even maliciously! – imagine that faith in Christ Jesus and delight in him are a little less important than they ought to be.

Look around instead for those whose constant confidence is Jesus Christ, whose constant boast is Jesus Christ, whose constant delight is Jesus Christ. Jesus is the centre of their worship, the centre of their gratitude, the centre of their love, the centre of their hope. After that, doubtless we shall sometimes need to argue about relatively peripheral matters. But in the first instance, emulate those whose constant confidence and boast are in Christ Jesus, and in nothing else.

Emulate those who are continuing to grow spiritually, not those who are stagnating (3:10–16)

Verse 10 is often cited by Christians today. What is astonishing is that it was first written by an apostle who had known Christ for almost thirty years. 'I want to know Christ', Paul writes – though of course he *does* know him. What he means is that he wants to know him better and better. If you love someone then you know that person, at least in measure. But your love for that person ensures you want to know that person more and more. A good marriage uncovers to the eyes of one spouse more and more about the other spouse, as long as that marriage endures.

That is the way Paul views Jesus. The riches bound up in him are unending. We shall spend all eternity getting to know him better, and we shall discover that knowing him is knowing God, and the exploration is eternal and inexhaustible. And already, during our pilgrimage here, it is our delight, as it is our duty, to know Jesus Christ better and better.

In particular, Paul says, 'I want to know Christ and the power of his resurrection and the fellowship of sharing in his sufferings, becoming like him in his death' (3:10). What does that mean?

In Paul's usage, the 'power of his resurrection' is the power of God that raised Jesus from the dead. According to Paul, that same 'incomparably great power' (Eph. 1:19), the power that raised Jesus from the dead, is the power that is at work in us to make us holy, to make us a fit place for Jesus to dwell in, to enable us to grasp the limitless dimensions of God's love for us (Eph. 3:14–19), to strengthen us so that we shall have great endurance and faith and lives constantly characterized by thanksgiving (Col. 1:11–12). It takes extraordinary power to change us to become like that. In fact, it takes nothing less than the power of God that raised Jesus from the dead. What the apostle wants, then, is not power so that we might be thought powerful, but power so that we might be conformed to the will of God. Only the power that brought Jesus back from death will do.

That is not all Paul wants. He wants 'the fellowship of sharing in [Christ's] sufferings' (3:10). Here again is the word 'fellowship' or 'partnership' that we considered in the first chapter. Paul wants to identify with Christ in his sufferings, to participate in those sufferings, to know Christ better by experiencing sufferings just as Jesus did. After all, this is the apostle who had earlier written, 'For it has been granted to you on behalf of Christ not only to believe on him, but also to suffer for him' (1:29). Clearly Paul is not the sort of leader who is prepared to tell his converts how to suffer but is unwilling to suffer himself.

We must see that there is no trace of spiritual masochism in this. Certainly Paul does not want to suffer simply because he likes to suffer, as if suffering gives him a kind of perverted joy, so he wants to suffer. Rather, Paul understands that the Master was 'a man of sorrows, and familiar with suffering' (Is. 53:3), and he feels it is part of knowing that Master that he should follow him. That means 'becoming like him in his death' (3:10) – that is, just as Jesus had been crucified, so also Paul wants to take up his cross and follow him. For the privilege of knowing that Master better, no suffering is too great.

Is it not obvious how adoption of the same stance would transform our witness and values? If Philippians 3:10 were our watchword, or if we like the first apostles learned to rejoice under persecution because we had been counted worthy of suffering disgrace for the Name (Acts 5:41), inevitably our own perspectives would change when we faced a whiff of opposition. We might say, 'Thank God! He is finally entrusting me with a little bit of persecution. I want more of it, if it means I may know Christ better.'

One reason Paul adopts this stance is that he holds the end in view: he wants to know Christ in these ways, he says, 'and so, somehow, to attain to the resurrection from the dead' (3:11). By this wording he does not mean to inject doubt as to whether or not he will himself attain the resurrection from the dead. The word 'somehow' in the original probably suggests that Paul is uncertain as to the timing and circumstances of this experience. Might it come to him in his lifetime, so that he receives a transformed, resurrection body without passing through death? We know from his first letter to the Thessalonians that that is what Paul teaches will befall those believers who are alive when Jesus returns (1 Thess.

4:13–17). Or will he die and then rise from the dead? Either way, 'somehow', he will 'attain to the resurrection from the dead'. And in Paul's mind, attaining that glorious end, the final resurrection, the new heaven and the new earth, the home of righteousness, is bound up with persevering in the knowledge of Jesus Christ. So for knowledge of Christ, Paul yearns.

In other words, Paul is not stagnating. And it is this attitude, more than any other, that ensures that when Paul tells us we are to imitate him (3:17; 1 Cor. 11:1) he is not setting himself up as a guru who has already 'arrived'. If Paul knows that he is a model to be imitated, he also knows that he is a model in transition to greater glory. If he wants to be followed, he wants to be followed not least in this, that he himself is still following hard after Jesus. He is pressing on. He does not think of himself as having already been made perfect. Indeed, he explicitly disavows the suggestion: 'Not that I have already obtained all this, or have already been made perfect, but I press on to take hold of that for which Christ Jesus took hold of me' (3:12). What he is aiming for is the attainment of the very purpose for which Christ called him. Anything less would be a betrayal of that calling.

As if the one disavowal is not enough, Paul repeats himself: 'Brothers, I do not consider myself yet to have taken hold of it. But one thing I do: Forgetting what is behind and straining toward what is ahead, I press on toward the goal to win the prize for which God has called me heavenwards in Christ Jesus' (3:13–14). Refusing to stand on past triumphs, Paul eagerly strains forward to the glories to come.

Not for a moment is Paul suggesting that his stance is unique, or one that is expected only of apostles. Far from it: 'All of us who are mature should take such a view of things' (3:15). This is how *any* mature Christian should think. And by implication, those who are immature should think this way, too: that is, they should become mature in order to think this way. That is why Paul adds, 'And if on some point you think differently, that too God will make clear to you' (3:15). And meanwhile, all Christians without exception should at least live up to the level of what they already know: 'Only let us live up to what we have already attained' (3:16).

The implications are staggering. Christians should never be satisfied with yesterday's grace. It is a shocking thing for Christians to have to admit that they have grown little in their knowledge of Jesus Christ. As Paul would later exhort Timothy, we are to be diligent in the Christian responsibilities laid on us, so that others may see our progress (1 Tim. 4:15). That includes both 'life' and 'doctrine' (1 Tim. 4:16).

Obviously these things apply with special urgency to preachers and teachers of the gospel. If you have been on the same plateau of both knowledge ('doctrine') and experience ('life') for the past twenty years, there is something dreadfully wrong. It is mandated of all of us that we grow: 'All of us who are mature should take such a view of things' (Phil. 3:15). It is not that we leave old truths and steps of holiness behind, but that new truths and applications of old truths open up before our eyes, and shape our knowledge and our living so powerfully that others see the improvement. Our sins become less and less excusable: those who are most saintly are invariably most deeply aware of how sinful they are, and how odious sin is to God. Holiness becomes more and more attractive. The glories of the world to come make all the glories of this world fade into dull greys by way of comparison.

Sadly, not all believers, not even all Christian leaders, adopt this stance that Paul views as normal and normative. So look around carefully, and emulate those who are continuing to grow spiritually, not those who are stagnating. Beware of those who project an image of smug self-satisfaction; imitate those who imitate Christ.

Emulate those who eagerly await Jesus' return, not those whose mind is on earthly things (3:17–21)

Verse 17 is transitional: it applies as well to what precedes as to what follows. Clearly, it brings to a focus what precedes. In case we have not discerned that Paul has talked so much about his own attitude toward growth and maturity precisely because he wants others to follow his pattern, he now makes the point explicitly: 'Join with others in following my example, brothers, and take note of those who live according to the pattern we gave you' (3:17). The 'others' to whom Paul refers are probably those in other churches. Paul's point is that he is not laying on the Philippians some special responsibility. If they follow Paul, they are doing no more than what Christians in other churches he has planted are doing. They are lining themselves up with other Christians in other centres. And since Paul cannot be everywhere at once, then they should carefully take note of Christians in their own number who live according to the pattern that Paul gave to the Philippian believers, and let them be their guide.

There are two unavoidable implications in this verse. (1) Part of what Paul taught new converts was how to live. He speaks of 'the pattern we gave you', which in the context clearly means the 'pattern of life (what we would call the "lifestyle") we gave you'. (2) Once again, the apostle assumes that many such elements in Christian discipleship are more easily caught than taught. That is why the Philippians are told to look around them for models, models who are clearly approximating to the apostolic model, and to follow them.

Equally clearly, verse 17 leads on to the thought of the last few verses of this chapter. By insisting that some of the believers make excellent models for others to follow, he implies that some others do not. 'For, as I have often told you before and now say again

even with tears, many live as enemies of the cross of Christ' (3:18).
But exactly who are these people?

It is hard to be certain and precise about their identity, but we
can draw some reasonable inferences. They are probably not self-
confessed unbelievers, for (1) it is unlikely that Paul would find
himself in tears over complete unbelievers who were danger-
ously likely to lead the Philippian believers astray; (2) in the
context, Paul is contrasting the model he and other mature
Christians provide with what these people are doing – and it is
unlikely that the Philippian Christians would be tempted to
model themselves after people who didn't at least make a claim
to being Christian; and (3) the expression 'enemies of the cross of
Christ' may suggest people who claim to be believers but who
are in reality 'fifth-column' enemies. The expression would surely
be unlikely if it referred to all unbelievers without distinction,
and if instead it referred to strong unbelievers who actively
opposed the gospel, then we return to the second point: it is
difficult to imagine why the Philippians would be tempted to
follow them.

It appears, then, that these people make some sort of profession of Christian faith, and draw away some, but in reality they
are 'enemies of the cross of Christ'. Every generation produces
some of these shysters. They are not to be confused with
Christian preachers whose motives may sometimes be mixed,
like those Paul mentions in 1:15–16. Nor are they to be confused
with pagans or others who make no pretence of faith in Christ,
but whose opposition to the gospel may become very intense.
Rather, they talk a good line, dupe the unwary and the undiscern-
ing, parade themselves as Christian leaders, and perhaps even
exhibit a good deal of 'power'. But what is missing, judging by
Paul's expression, is a focus on the cross like his own: Paul wants
to know more both of the power of Christ's resurrection *and of*

the fellowship of sharing in his sufferings, becoming like him in his death (3:11). Enemies of the cross of Christ never adopt that stance.

Doubtless who these people are was clear both to Paul and to the Philippians. Paul adds enough details to enable the first readers to make a clear identification: 'Their destiny is destruction' – that is, they are not real believers, however much they say otherwise. Further, 'their god is their stomach, and their glory is in their shame': far from being drawn to suffering for Christ's sake, they are endlessly drawn to creature comforts. They please themselves; their god is located no higher than their belly. The kinds of things they really value, far from being inspiring and glorious and worthy of emulation, are downright shameful. In brief, 'Their mind is on earthly things' (3:19). It is not that they focus on explicitly wicked things. But if all of their values and cherished goals are tied to what belongs to this world and this earth, and no part of them breathes, with the passion of Paul, 'somehow, to attain to the resurrection from the dead' (3:11), they are to be pitied. Certainly they are to be avoided, so far as any modelling is concerned.

Paul's vigorous denunciation is not callous or spiteful. He issues it 'even with tears' (3:18). He is grieved to find professing Christian leaders who in fact are idolaters ('their god is their belly') and wretchedly lost ('their destiny is destruction'). We are reminded of the tears of Christ, whom Paul is emulating. When Jesus denounces the religious charlatans of his day, he ends up in grief as he looks over the city (Matt. 23). For our part, we must not become people who denounce but who do not weep. Neither may we become people who weep but who never denounce. Too much is at stake both ways.

In any case, Paul insists that genuine Christians cannot adopt the stances of these enemies of Christ. By contrast with them,

Paul insists, 'our citizenship is in heaven. And we eagerly await a Saviour from there, the Lord Jesus Christ, who, by the power that enables him to bring everything under his control, will transform our lowly bodies so that they will be like his glorious body' (3:20–21). Paul insists in the strongest terms that genuine Christianity, the kind that he wants imitated, lives in the light of Jesus' return. It is Christianity that joins the church in every generation, crying, 'Amen. Come, Lord Jesus!' (Rev. 22:20).

In short, it is Christianity that is *preparing* for heaven, for that is where our true home is, our true citizenship, our true destiny. Only that stance is sufficient to make Paul's attitude toward suffering sensible and reasonable. If cheerful identification with Christ and his sufferings in this world finally issues in the spectacular glory of the Lord's return and the splendour that follows, then we, too, are vindicated, in a fashion somewhat analogous to the way that Christ was vindicated (see on 2:6–11).

Genuine spirituality cannot long outlive an attitude that is homesick for heaven, that lives with eternity's values in view, that eagerly awaits Jesus' return, that anticipates the day when Christ himself will 'bring everything under his control' and 'will transform our lowly bodies so that they will be like his glorious body' (a theme Paul treats more fully in 1 Corinthians 15). Thoughtful Christians will not see themselves first of all as citizens of the United Kingdom or the US or Canada or Pago Pago. We are citizens of heaven. Only that citizenship has enduring significance. Happy the believer whose epitaph was the couplet:

Of this blessed man let this praise be given:
Heaven was in him before he was in heaven.

Emulate those who eagerly await Jesus' return, not those whose mind is on earthly things.

Cotton Mather, an American Puritan of great influence and learning in his day, wrote:

> Examples do strangely charm us into imitation. When holiness is pressed upon us we are prone to think that it is a doctrine calculated for angels and spirits whose dwelling is not with flesh. But when we read the lives of them that excelled in holiness, though they were persons of like passions with ourselves, the conviction is wonderful and powerful.

But of course, there is a sting in the tail of all that I have written in this chapter. I have cast it all in terms of our responsibility to emulate worthy Christian leaders, and then followed the text in discovering the characteristics of these worthy Christian leaders. But if we Christians are responsible for finding suitable examples whom we might properly emulate, *then of course when we do so we shall become suitable examples whom others will emulate.*

Not all ministry in the church is verbal; not all ministry is prominent. But all Christians are called upon to set a standard of talk and life that influences a new generation of converts in a godly and Christ-honouring way.

In some senses, the needs are becoming more urgent. There are rising numbers of Christian families that have given no thought to family devotions. Who will model for them what is to be done? Homes are ripped apart by divorce: which Christian parents will model for a new generation of young people, sometimes brought up with little love or with confusing models, what a Christian marriage looks like? It is common knowledge that abusive people are often the offspring of abusive people: will we not simultaneously proclaim the gospel and model what generous, self-denying, content, Christian homes look like? Christians used to be known as those who know how to die well: will we not show a new generation of believers how to die, how to grieve, how to trust, how to disagree with another believer without turning belligerent and while still cherishing forbearance and humility? Will we show by our example how to stand up for righteousness in our society? Did we not learn to pray by listening to others? Whom, then, have we taught to pray? Whom have we taught the rudiments of self-discipline?

Yes, we must emulate those who are interested in the wellbeing of others, and not their own; but we must be such people ourselves. Yes, we must emulate those who have proved themselves in hardship, not the untested upstart and the self-promoting peacock; but we must become such people. Yes, we must emulate those whose constant confidence and boast are in Christ Jesus, and nothing else; but that must be our boast, too. Yes, we must emulate those who are continuing to grow spiritually, not those who are stagnating; but of course, if we do, we shall grow ourselves. Yes, we must emulate those who eagerly await Jesus' return, not those whose mind is on earthly things; but then our minds will be on heavenly things, no less than theirs. And we shall look out on a new generation whom we may influence for Jesus' sake. That is the mandate: to go and make disciples.

Brothers and sisters in Christ, we are called to emulate worthy Christian leaders. We are called to be worthy Christian leaders whom others will emulate.

God help us.

Never give up the Christian walk

Philippians 4:1–23

In working through Paul's letter to the believers in Philippi, we have summarized his argument in several simple formulas:

1. Put the gospel first.
2. Adopt Jesus' death as a test of your outlook.
3. Emulate worthy Christian leaders.
   And now,
4. Never give up the Christian walk.

But why should this last imperative be made the summary of Philippians 4? There are at least three reasons.

First, the burden of the first verse is to 'stand firm', and this verse is transitional, pointing both backwards to what we have already examined, and forward to the chapter ahead. Paul writes, 'Therefore, my brothers, you whom I love and long for, my joy and crown, that is how you should stand firm in the Lord, dear friends!' The evidence

that this verse points backward is clear enough: *'Therefore*, my brothers . . .*': that is, in the light of the themes just articulated, especially in
the light of 3:17 ('Join with others in following my example . . .'), *therefore* stand firm. Indeed, Paul injects a tender, emotional element: 'my
brothers', he addresses them, 'you whom I love and long for, my joy
and crown'. He has warned them about false leaders, bad examples.
Watch out for those who parade a pseudo-Christianity that may for a
while take you in. Beware of those whose god is their belly and
whose end is destruction. Do not be deceived by them. Imitate
instead those worthy Christian leaders who make much of the cross,
and whose spiritual life is vital, growing, and constantly focused on
Jesus Christ. In particular, in the light of the Lord's impending
return, when he will even transform our bodies, *therefore* stand firm.

So the way 4:1 points backward is clear enough. But there is
also a word in this verse that almost certainly points forward. If I
were rendering the verse in a crassly literal way, part of it would
read *'thus* stand firm in the Lord' (rendered *'that is how* you should
stand firm in the Lord' in the NIV). The word I have rendered 'thus'
regularly points forward. For example, a literal rendering of John
3:16 reads, 'For God *thus* loved the world that he gave his one and
only Son': the word 'thus' points forward to the supreme evidence
that God loved the world. So also here in Philippians 4:1: *'thus*
stand firm' – that is, stand firm in the way I am about to prescribe.
Stand firm; never give up the Christian walk.

Secondly, many of the themes in Philippians 4 have already
been treated in Philippians 1–3. But in this last chapter of Paul's
letter, these themes are recast in such a way as to foster perseverance and endurance. This will become abundantly clear as we
work our way through the chapter. So this becomes an additional
reason for treating the chapter under this theme.

Thirdly, most importantly of all, we cannot help but see that
many of the specific injunctions in this chapter are calculated to

foster perseverance. What Paul offers is not simply doctrinal content (though that is important) or simple orders designed to elicit some sort of explicitly Christian behaviour, but attitudinal commands aimed at fostering whole-life, long-lasting commitment to the one true God.

We may put it this way. What kind of exhortation will best help Christians persevere in the way of Christ? Should we encourage one another to recite the creeds and read our Bibles more? Certainly we should – but we must also acknowledge that one can treat the Bible coldly, or merely as an object of academic pursuit (in much the same way as others study Shakespeare). Shall we foster obedience to specific commandments? Yes, doubtless we all need encouragement along those lines from time to time. Yet some obedience is merely formal; other kinds of obedience sink into a pathetic brand of legalism.

So the kinds of things Paul chooses to emphasize in his closing chapter are these: integrity in relationships, fidelity toward God, quiet confidence in him, purity and wholesomeness in thought, godliness in heart attitude. In every area, Paul wants to foster firmness, stability, endurance, perseverance, faithfulness before God – before the God who has disclosed himself so wonderfully and climactically in Jesus Christ, his Son.

The burden of Philippians 4, then, is this: never give up the Christian walk. We may usefully unpack this theme and discover seven components.

Resolve to pursue like-mindedness with other true believers (4:2–3)

The concrete case immediately before Paul concerns two women, Euodia and Syntyche, who cannot seem to get along. What is shocking in this situation is that these two are not peripheral people known for their bad tempers and wagging tongues, and for little else. No, they are women who have worked with Paul in the cause of the gospel (4:3). They have been at the forefront of evangelism: they 'have contended at my side in the cause of the gospel', Paul writes. There is no hint of heresy or immorality in them; they simply cannot get on. So what does Paul do?

First, he pleads with them. Isn't that wonderful? He does not begin with heavy-handed authority. He does not cite his apostolic credentials and tear a strip off them. Indeed, for all that the appeal is personal and impassioned, it is not calculated to shame them. There are important lessons to be learned here for those who are called to mediate in contemporary personality conflicts within the church.

Secondly, Paul asks the person who is to receive this letter to intervene and help the two women sort it out. Sometimes frictions between believers become so severe that the wise course is for a third party to mediate between the two sides and try to help each side see things from the other's perspective, and think through what faithful Christian attitudes should be in such circumstances. Who the person is in this case we do not know. When a letter was sent to the entire local church, as this letter was, doubtless it had to be sent more specifically to an individual who would read it to the whole church. Certainly Paul and the Philippian church knew who this individual was, but we do not. It is reasonable to assume that this person was an elder, a pastor; it may even have been Luke. But we cannot be certain. In fact, it is even possible that the word rendered 'yoke-fellow' is a proper name (though there is no independent attestation of such a name in the ancient world). In that case, by referring to the man as (literally) 'true Yoke-fellow', Paul is resorting to a pun: Mr Yoke-fellow in name and true yoke-fellow in action, as you are yoked together with me in the cause of the gospel. But whoever this person is, Paul asks him to intervene.

Thirdly, the substance of Paul's plea to the women, and the aim of the intervention he wants from his 'loyal yoke-fellow', is that the two women 'agree with each other in the Lord'. The verb translated 'to agree with' is a common one in Philippians, appearing no fewer than ten times in these four short chapters. What exactly is Paul asking for?

(1) This is not an appeal for unity at the expense of truth. Paul does not say, 'Regardless of what is coming between you, bury the hatchet. Do not ever let doctrine stand in the way of unanimity. Doctrine does not matter; just love one another, and that will be enough.' The Paul who thinks doctrinal matters can draw a line between the person who is reconciled to God and the person who is anathema (Gal. 1:8–9) is unlikely to be slipping into relativistic sentimentality here. When fundamental gospel interests are at stake, it is sometimes necessary to divide. But that is not what is going on here in Philippi.

(2) In the light of the argument of Philippians as a whole, this is not a hopeless demand for perfect agreement on every subject. Paul is not saying to Euodia and Syntyche, 'Ladies, on every single point of doctrine and life I expect you to thrash out your differences and arrive at perfect agreement.' For when the verb is used elsewhere, the appeal is broader and deeper. Recall, after all, Paul's argument at the beginning of Philippians 2. 'If you have any encouragement from being united with Christ, if any comfort from his love, . . . if any tenderness and compassion, then make my joy complete *by being like-minded* [same verb], *having the same love, being one in spirit and purpose*' (2:1–2). In other words, Paul is appealing for a mental attitude that adopts the same basic direction as other believers, the same fundamental aim, the same orientation and priorities. This is a *gospel* orientation.

Some honest differences of opinion among genuine believers could be resolved if they would take the time to sort out *why* they are looking at things differently, if they would take their views and attitudes and submit them afresh, self-critically, to the Scriptures. But many disputes will not be resolved because those who are quarrelling will neither take the time nor deploy the energy to study the Scriptures together. In some cases, neither side *wants* to be corrected or sharpened: both sides are so convinced they are right that mere facts will not correct them, and in any case all they want to do is win. In that frame of mind, they easily forget that it is always inappropriate at best, and frankly sinful at worst, to try to manipulate believers into changing their minds. You know the kind of comments I have in mind: 'Your stance hurts my feelings. Don't you trust me?' Emotional blackmail is never a mark of godliness. It is never a sign of Christian maturity when, under the guise of preserving good relations, Christians try to manipulate others. Usually what is being exposed is a rather embarrassing immaturity. Where there are disagreements of principle, argue them out. Take out your Bibles, think things through, find out why you are disagreeing, be willing to be corrected.

But in *every* case, whether you can reach agreement on this detail or that, identify what takes absolute priority, and begin with that. Focus on what you have in common. Make sure you agree over the gospel. Work hard to develop perfect agreement on matters of greatest importance: the gospel, the Word of God, the glory of Christ, the good of God's people, the beauty of holiness, the ugliness of sin, especially your own. Personal differences should never become an occasion for advancing your party, for stroking bruised egos, for resorting to cheap triumphalism, for trimming the gospel by appealing to pragmatics. Focus on what unites you: the gospel, the gospel, the gospel. Be like-minded; think the same things; agree with one another. Work hard and humbly on these central issues, and in most instances the peripheral matters will take care of themselves. Resolve to pursue like-mindedness with other believers. This will ennoble and strengthen all sides, so that you will never abandon the Christian walk.

Resolve always to rejoice in the Lord (4:4)

Paul writes, 'Rejoice in the Lord always. I will say it again: Rejoice!' (4:4). Of course, Paul has already introduced this theme into his letter. In the first chapter, Paul assured his readers, 'In all my prayers for all of you, I always pray *with joy* because of your partnership in the gospel' (1:4–5a). The theme recurs in chapter 2: Paul is ready to be poured out as a kind of drink offering, a sacrifice on top of all their sacrifices – and if this should transpire he would be glad and rejoice with them, and expect them to be glad and rejoice with him (2:17–18). The same theme is picked up in chapter 3: 'So then, my brothers, rejoice in the Lord!' (3:1). And now it returns once more, and in a most emphatic form.

Doubtless the Philippians could not read many such exhortations from the apostle without remembering that Paul had been a prime example of this virtue when he had first preached the gospel among them. According to Acts 16, he and Silas were arrested and thrown into prison. Beaten, bruised, their feet in stocks, they displayed not a whiff of self-pity. Far from it: they began a midnight chorus of praise. Now Paul finds himself in prison again. He is not writing this epistle from a chalet in the south of France, or taking a few minutes out from the happy pleasures of paddling in the waters off Tenerife. He is under arrest. And what does he say? 'Hang in there, brothers and sisters, as I am trying to hang on myself'? Not a chance! 'Rejoice in the Lord. I will say it again: Rejoice!'

In one sense, this injunction is so self-evidently right that it is embarrassing that we should have to be reminded of it. Surely all redeemed men and women will want to rejoice in the Lord. Our sins have been forgiven! We have been declared righteous, because another has borne our guilt. We have received the gift of the Spirit, the down-payment of the promised inheritance that will be ours when Jesus comes again. We are children of the living God. Our 'threescore years and ten' may be fraught with difficulty, but eternity awaits us, secured by the Son of God. We shall see Christ face to face, and spend an eternity in the purest worship and in consummated holiness. If we fail to respond with joy and gratitude when we are reminded of these things, it is either because we have not properly grasped the depth of the abyss of our own sinful natures and of the curse from which we have been freed by Jesus, or we have not adequately glimpsed the splendour of the heights to which we have been raised.

Happy, then, the believer who can repeat David's words with renewed understanding, 'He lifted me out of the slimy pit, out of the mud and mire; he set my feet on a rock and gave me a firm place to stand. He put a new song in my mouth, a hymn of praise to our God' (Ps. 40:2–3). Happy the Christian who sees in every sin a monster that could easily snare him eternally, were it not for the grace of God. Small wonder, then, that Peter writes, 'Though you have not seen him, you love him; and even though you do not see him now, you believe in him and are filled *with an inexpressible and glorious joy*, for you are receiving the goal of your faith, the salvation of your souls' (1 Pet. 1:8–9). The kingdom of God may be entered through suffering (Acts 14:22), but it is characterized by joy: Paul insists that 'the kingdom of God is not a matter of eating and drinking', that is, of obeying rules and observing kosher food laws, 'but of righteousness, peace and joy in the Holy Spirit, because anyone who serves Christ in this way is pleasing to God and approved by men' (Rom. 14:17–18).

But note some details in the text.

First, we are exhorted to rejoice *in the Lord*. The controlling issue is not the style of rejoicing, but the ground. We are not necessarily rejoicing in the Lord because we are boisterous and loud and uninhibited in a large conference hall where the singing is swinging. Such praise may in some instances be entirely appropriate; equally, joy in the Lord may be happily expressed in solemn silence, in tears of gratitude, in sheer delight in times of prayer. But Paul's focus is not on the style; it is on the ground of the rejoicing.

That means the ultimate ground of our rejoicing can never be our circumstances, even though we recognize, as Christians, that our circumstances are providentially arranged. If our joy derives primarily from our circumstances, then when our circumstances change we will be miserable. Our delight must be in the Lord himself. That is what enables us to live with joy *above* our circumstances. As Nehemiah puts it, 'the joy of the LORD is your strength' (Neh. 8:10). Perhaps that is one of the reasons the Lord sometimes allows miserable circumstances to lash us. Perhaps that is why James, the half-brother of our Lord, wisely counsels, 'Consider it pure joy, my brothers, whenever you face trials of many kinds, because you know that the testing of your faith develops perseverance. Perseverance must finish its work so that you may be mature and complete, not lacking anything' (Jas. 1:2–3). Whatever the mysteries of evil and sorrow, they do have the salutary effect of helping believers to shift the ground of their joy from created things to the Creator, from the temporary to the eternal, from jingoism to Jesus, from consumption to God. As the song puts it, 'He washed my eyes with tears, that I might see.'

Secondly, the text implicitly answers two questions: (1) *When* are we to rejoice in the Lord? And (2) *for how long?* To both questions, the text answers with one word: always. 'Rejoice in the Lord *always.*' And this is a command, not simply good advice. Obedience to this command is possible because the ground of this rejoicing is changeless. Our circumstances may rightly call from us grief, tears, sorrow. Unless the Lord comes back first, each of us will face death – our own, and, if we live long enough, the death of loved ones and friends. And we will weep. But even in our tears, we may rejoice, we will rejoice, we must rejoice, for we rejoice in the Lord. He does not change. And that is why we shall rejoice in the Lord *always.*

God well knows that a believer who conscientiously obeys this command cannot be a backbiter or a gossip. Such a believer cannot be spiritually proud or filled with conceit, cannot be stingy or prayerless, cannot be a chronic complainer or perpetually bitter. The cure for a crushed and bitter spirit is to see Christ Jesus the Lord, and then to rejoice in him. Lurking and nourished sins are always a sign that our vision of Jesus is dim, and our joy in him has evaporated with the morning dew. By contrast, the believer who practises rejoicing in the Lord increasingly discovers balm in the midst of heartache, rest in the midst of exhausting tension, love in the midst of loneliness, and the presence of God in control of excruciating circumstances. Such a believer never gives up the Christian walk. Resolve always to rejoice in the Lord.

Resolve to be known for gentleness (4:5)

That is what Paul commands: 'Let your gentleness be evident to all. The Lord is near' (4:5).

The word rendered 'gentleness' in the NIV is not easy to translate. Some older versions offer 'forbearance', which isn't bad. It refers to the exact opposite of a spirit of contention and self-seeking, which is why the NIV opts for 'gentleness'. But this gentleness must not be confused with being a wimp, with the kind of person whose personality is akin to a wet dishcloth. What is in view is a certain kind of willed, self-effacing kindness.

That suggests that there is some irony in Paul's exhortation. We crystallize it if we over-translate: 'Be known for being self-effacing.' The pedant might urge that being self-effacing precludes the desire to be known; trying to be known for something surely rules out being known for being self-effacing. But now we are close to the point Paul is making.

What do most of us want to be known for? Do you want to be known for your extraordinary good looks? Do you want to be known for your quick wit? For your sense of humour, or your sagacity? Do you want to be known for your wealth, for your family connections? Or perhaps you are more pious, and want to be known for your prayer life, or for your excellent skills as a leader of inductive Bible studies. Many a preacher wants to be known for his preaching.

How appalling. The sad fact is that even our highest and best motives are so easily corroded by self-interest that we begin to overlook this painful reality. Paul cuts to the heart of the issue: be known for gentleness.

The self-sins are tricky things, damnably treacherous. In one of his books, A. W. Tozer writes:

> To be specific, the self-sins are these: self-righteousness, self-pity, self-confidence, self-sufficiency, self-admiration, self-love, and a host of others like them. They dwell too deep within us and are too much a part of our natures to come to our attention till the light of God is focused upon them. The grosser manifestations of these sins, egotism, exhibitionism, self-promotion, are strangely tolerated in Christian leaders, even in circles

of impeccable orthodoxy . . . Promoting self under the guise of promoting Christ is currently so common as to excite little notice . . .

That was written over half a century ago. What would Tozer say now? He goes on:

Self can live unrebuked at the very altar. It can watch the bleeding Victim die and not be in the least affected by what it sees. It can fight for the faith of the Reformers and preach eloquently the creed of salvation by grace, and gain strength by its efforts. To tell all the truth, it seems actually to feed upon orthodoxy and is more at home in a Bible conference than in a tavern. Our very state of longing after God may afford it an excellent condition under which to thrive and grow.[7]

It is so very easy to mistake the genuine movement of the Spirit for assorted counterfeits. Or perhaps more difficult yet is the movement where there is something genuinely of God, and not a little of the flesh. In the nineteenth century in America, there were many 'camp revivals'. These were evangelistic and holiness meetings aimed at calling people to repentance. On the American frontier, they were often very well attended. Doubtless they were a means of blessing to many. But a rather painful study has shown that nine months after many of these 'camp revivals' there was a very high illegitimacy rate. Isn't that remarkable? One can understand why. There was such a spirit of friendship and camaraderie and closeness, that intimacy in one arena spilled over into intimacy in another, until one of the fruits of 'camp revivals' was a disproportionately high illegitimacy rate. Surely that was not of God!

One of the tests that can be applied to determine whether a movement is of God – though certainly it is not the only one – is to observe to what degree those affected are making it their aim to be known for gentleness. In this, they are becoming like their Master. Is that not one of the lessons made clear in chapter 2 of this epistle? 'Your attitude should be the same as that of Christ Jesus', Paul insists – and then outlines how this Jesus, though he enjoyed equality with God, did not view such equality as something to be exploited, but made himself nothing, became a human being, and died the ignominious and shameful death of crucifixion. He became known for selflessness.

May God grant that all who read these pages will pray earnestly for this virtue, and resolve steadily to pursue it. For such believers will never be moved; they will never give up the Christian walk.

Sometimes we sing these things better than we live them:

May the Word of God dwell richly
   In my heart from hour to hour,
So that all may see I triumph
   Only through his power.

May the love of Jesus fill me
   As the waters fill the sea;
Him exalting, self abasing,
   This is victory.

May his beauty rest upon me
   As I seek the lost to win,
And may they forget the channel,
   Seeing only him.
(Kate Barclay Wilkinson)

Resolve to be known for gentleness.

Paul gives us a specific reason for obeying this injunction. 'Let your gentleness be evident to all', he writes, and then adds, 'The

Lord is near' (4:5). This could mean one of two things. Both make sense; I am not quite certain which the apostle means.

Paul could mean that the Lord is near *temporally*, that is, that he is coming soon. In that case, the argument runs like this. In the light of the impending return of the Lord Jesus (to which urgent reference was made at the end of Philippians 3), there is more than a little incentive to be gentle and selfless. The Lord's return provides incentive. As the apostle John writes elsewhere, 'Everyone who has this hope [*i.e.* the hope of the Lord's return and of our transformation at that time] in him [either 'in himself', *i.e.* in the believer, or 'in Christ', referring to the object of the hope] purifies himself, just as he is pure' (1 John 3:3).

What would you like to be doing when Jesus comes again?

What would you like to be saying when Jesus comes again?

What would you like to be thinking when Jesus comes again?

Each of us can readily think of what we would *not* like to be doing or saying or thinking when Jesus comes again. When I was a boy in Sunday School we sang the chorus:

Doing good deeds, sowing good seed,
Leaving life's follies behind me;
Doing my best, standing each test –
That's how I want the Lord to find me.

'Let your gentleness be evident to all. The Lord is *near.*'

That is one way of reading the second part of this verse (4:5). But because of the particular expressions that Paul uses, I suspect it is marginally more likely that Paul means that the Lord is near *spatially* or perhaps better *personally*. He is not far off; he is very near. How then can we give ourselves to self-promotion?

Suppose, for a moment, that the resurrected and exalted Lord were to walk into the room where you and your friends were seated. Suppose that there were no doubt in anyone's mind as to his identity. How would you respond? Would you immediately rush up to him and strut your excellence? As he showed you a glimpse of his glory, and turned over his nail-scarred hands, would you be quick to parade your virtues? Would self-promotion play any part in your thinking at that point?

Not a chance! But that is the point: the Lord Jesus has promised to be present, by his Spirit, where even two or three of his disciples gather in his name. Does it change the fundamental reality simply because we cannot at the moment see him?

'Let your gentleness be evident to all. The Lord is *near*.'

Resolve not to be anxious about anything, but learn instead to pray (4:6–7)

This is perhaps the most striking resolution so far, yet it is nothing but a paraphrase of Paul's own words: 'Do not be anxious about anything, but in everything, by prayer and petition, with thanksgiving, present your requests to God' (4:6).

There is a sense in which our society demands that we worry on a broader scale than any society in the history of the race. If we were to travel back, say, eight hundred years or so, we would discover that most people in Europe worried about nothing more than local matters. Of course, those local matters could be severe: medical help was not impressive, most families lost one or more children, life could be harsh, brutal, and short. But communication with other parts of the world was difficult and late. Most people gave little thought to what people were doing in the next county, let alone the next country or the next continent. Apart from extraordinary events, like the Crusades, when your local feudal lord might sweep you up and carry you off to war, you were not called upon to worry about the international scene. Even national news that could affect you was late and essentially alien. The overwhelming majority of people could scarcely visualize their monarch, for of course no pictures or photographs were printed and circulated.

Then came the printing press. It was followed by the telegraph. Alexander Bell invented the telephone; Marconi invented the radio. Not that long ago we started decorating the sky with satellites. My E-mail exchanges with a colleague in, say, Papua New Guinea, bounce off a reflector twenty-two thousand miles out in space. But the result of these greatly improved communications, of course, is that we now speak of the 'global village'. A few shots can be fired almost anywhere in the world, and if in the opinion of the news editors nothing of greater significance has happened to claim prime-time television, the entire episode will be replayed tonight on the evening news, inviting your worry.

So our advances in communications demand that we worry about peace, economics, famine in the Sahel, enormous disparities of wealth in Latin America and the Philippines, cultural decline in the West, the breakup of the Soviet empire, civil conflict in the Balkans, genocide in Rwanda, and on and on.

Of course, our worries are not limited to international affairs. Personal and cultural problems are constantly polled, demographically checked, statistically analysed, and paraded in our newspapers and on our televisions. Then the economy changes, and suddenly very few have permanent jobs, and some of us do not have any jobs at all. Then of course we can add up the regular parade of pressures: car troubles, conflict with colleagues at work, impending exams and the expectations that family and friends impose, competition at work, a degenerating family, an arid marriage, a rebellious teenager, bereavement, financial insecurity. Pressures mount and surround us and bully us, until even the

Christian who hears the injunction of this passage ('Do not be anxious about anything') smiles half-bitterly and mutters, 'You don't understand; it can't be done.'

But of course, it can be. Part of our problem is that we encounter this command not to worry, perhaps in a conference or in a book, and we smile piously, grit our teeth, resolve not to worry, and promptly begin to worry about not worrying. What we overlook is that Scripture here tells us *how* to overcome our anxieties. 'Do not be anxious about anything' is not a naked prohibition; the alternative is immediately provided: '. . . but in everything, by prayer and petition, with thanksgiving, present your requests to God' (4:6).

Those of us who have been born into the family of God know about these things. But knowing about them and finding them true in our experience are two different things. When was the last time you prayed explicitly and at length over the things that worry you, trouble you, plague you? Did you take them out and recount them to God, one by one, laying your burdens on him?

Time. Time alone and still before God. That is what we need. Our lives are so rushed that we begrudge a three-minute 'quiet time', and then we wonder where God is. Yet the psalmist had it right: 'He who dwells in the shelter of the Most High will rest in the shadow of the Almighty. I will say of the LORD, "He is my refuge and my fortress, my God, in whom I trust"' (Ps. 91:1–2). Christians who come before the Father in regular prayer discover that Peter is right: 'Cast all your anxiety on him because he cares for you' (1 Pet. 5:7). They discover that Paul is right: 'And we know that in all things God works for the good of those who love him, who have been called according to his purpose' (Rom. 8:28). We are refreshed in the assurance of God's sovereign and wise goodness. According to Philippians 4, the way to be anxious about nothing is to be prayerful about everything: '*in everything*, by prayer and petition . . . present your requests to God'. Bengel was right to insist that anxiety and genuine prayer are more opposed to each other than fire and water. I have yet to meet a chronic worrier who enjoys an excellent prayer life.

> Ye fearful saints, fresh courage take;
>   The clouds ye so much dread
> Are big with mercy, and shall break
>   In blessings on your head.
>
> Judge not the Lord by feeble sense,
>   But trust him for his grace;
> Behind a frowning providence
>   He hides a smiling face.
>
> His purposes will ripen fast,
>   Unfolding every hour;
> The bud may have a bitter taste,
>   But sweet will be the flower.
>
> Blind unbelief is sure to err,
>   And scan his work in vain;
> God is his own interpreter,
>   And he will make it plain.
> (William Cowper)

None of this should be misconstrued as a 'Pollyanna-ish' approach to life. Christians are not ostriches, heads carefully buried in the sand. None of this means that our paths will be smooth, their borders lined with the sweetest-smelling roses. There is no hint that we shall live above the pressures of other mortals because we escape them.

Far from it. It is precisely in the context of the pressures all must endure that we find our rest in God. If you worry little simply because Providence has so far blessed you with a relatively easy course through life, or if you worry little because you have a carefree personality, you know little of the truth of this passage. This passage does not deny the existence of anxieties; it tells us what to do with them. It does not tell us that if you have the right personality you can live above tension; it tells us where we find strength and grace to help in times of need.

In fact, we are to go on the offensive. Not only are we to present our prayers and petitions to God, we are to do so 'with thanksgiving'. This, surely, is what is elsewhere called 'a sacrifice of praise' (Heb. 13:15). Any twit can offer praise when things are going well. To praise when by common human reckoning everything is the pits – this is what demands the sacrifice of praise. In Philippians 4, Paul insists that this must be our constant policy: along with our petitions and cares, we offer our heavenly Father thanksgiving. For in fact, even in the most extreme sorrow and distress, there is much for which to give thanks to God – above all, the privilege of being reconciled to him by the death of his dear Son, and all the blessings that come our way, in this life and in the next, because of this great salvation.

Resolve not to be anxious about anything, but learn instead to pray.

The result, as Paul describes it, is lovely: 'And the peace of God, which transcends all understanding, will guard your hearts and your minds in Christ Jesus' (Phil. 4:7). Once gain it is clear that Paul does not expect that the answer to our prayers will most likely take us out of the problems, but that our hearts and minds will be garrisoned by the peace of God. This is not some easily analysed bit of clever psychology. At the end of the day, it 'transcends all understanding': it is part of well-known Christian experience, as many who read these pages can attest, and it must not be reduced to a bit of clever suggestion or escapist comfort. God's peace stabilizes us, guards us, suffusing us with the joy of the Lord. Christians delight in trusting him.

In the words of a Scottish preacher from the nineteenth century:

> I stand upon the mount of God
>   With sunlight in my soul;
> I hear the storms in vales beneath,
>   I hear the thunders roll.
>
> But I am calm with thee, my God,
>   Beneath these glorious skies;
> And to the height on which I stand
>   No storms, no clouds can rise.
>
> O, this is life! O this is joy,
>   My God, to find thee so:
> Thy face to see, thy voice to hear,
>   And all thy love to know.
> (Horatius Bonar)

Or again,

> Drop thy still dews of quietness,
>   Till all our strivings cease;
> Take from our souls the strain and stress,
> And let our ordered lives confess
>   The beauty of thy peace.
>
> Breathe through the heats of our desire
>   Thy coolness and thy balm.

Let sense be dumb, let flesh retire;
Speak through the earthquake, wind, and fire,
   O still small voice of calm!
(J. G. Whittier)

Resolve not to be anxious about anything, but learn instead to pray. Nothing will prove so effective in strengthening your spiritual stamina, in giving you grace never to give up the Christian walk.

Resolve to think holy thoughts (4:8–9)

That, surely, is what Paul means: 'Finally, brothers, whatever is true, whatever is noble, whatever is right, whatever is pure, whatever is lovely, whatever is admirable – if anything is excellent or praiseworthy – think about such things' (4:8).

It always makes me fearful to remember that God knows my thoughts. Hebrews 4:13 reminds us, 'Nothing in all creation is hidden from God's sight. Everything is uncovered and laid bare before the eyes of him to whom we must give account.' Small wonder that David, after his sin with Bathsheba, could write, 'Search me, O God, and know my heart. Test me and know my anxious thoughts. See if there is any offensive way in me, and lead me in the way everlasting' (Ps. 139:23–24).

Clearly, David recognized not only that God *knew* his thoughts, but that any real reform in his life must *begin with* his thoughts. That is why the Lord Jesus taught, in the Sermon on the Mount, that murder can be traced to hate, and adultery to lust (Matt. 5:43–47, 27–30). That is also why, from God's perspective, the real measure of individuals lies in what they think: not in what they own, or in how well they deploy their gifts, or even in what they do, but in what they think. If you think holy thoughts, you will be holy; if you think garbage, you will be garbage.

So it should come as no surprise that the prophets insist, 'Let the wicked forsake his way *and the evil man his thoughts*' (Is. 55:7). One of the sovereign remedies against sin is to spend much time, thoughtful time, meditative time, in the Scriptures, for it is impossible to get rid of the trash in our minds without replacing it with an entirely different way of thinking. Even kings and leaders, extraordinarily busy people, are told to make this their first priority (*e.g.* Deut. 17:18–20; Josh. 1:7–9). On the night he was betrayed, Jesus prayed for his followers in these terms: 'Sanctify them by the truth; your word is truth' (John 17:17). There is no enduring sanctification apart from the truth of the gospel taking hold of our minds. The way we avoid being conformed to this world, the way we are transformed into conformity with Christ, is by the renewing of our minds (Rom. 12:2).

I know it is possible for people to gain a sort of mechanical knowledge of Scripture that is not characterized by repentance and faith, and therefore remains spiritually fruitless. But for most of us, that is not our current danger. Our current danger is that we make very little effort to think God's thoughts after him, to hide his word in our heart that we might not sin against him (Ps. 119:11). To hide God's word in our hearts, as opposed to our computers, means we ought to memorize it, read and re-read it, think about it, turn it over in our minds. Only such committed absorption of what God says will enable us in turn to confront and change the unbiblical worldviews all around us – or, as Paul puts it, to 'demolish arguments and every pretension that sets itself up against the knowledge of God' and to 'take captive every thought to make it obedient to Christ' (2 Cor. 10:5).

In the passage before us, Paul puts things in the most concrete way. Think about true things, Paul insists, not about the false.

Think about noble things, not the base. Think about whatever is right; do not dwell on the wrong. (What does this say about the programmes you watch on television?) Think about whatever is pure, not the sleazy. Think about the lovely, not the disgusting. Think about the admirable, not the despicable. Whatever is excellent, think about it.

This is not some escapist demand to avoid the harsh realities of our fallen world. The sad fact is that many people dwell on dirt without grasping that it *is* dirt. The wise Christian will see plenty of dirt in the world, but will recognize it *as* dirt, precisely because everything that is clean has captured his or her mind.

The hymnwriter was right:

Guide my thoughts, keep them from straying
Into paths unwise for me,
Lest I should, thy love betraying,
Turn aside from Calvary.

Or again:

May the mind of Christ my Saviour
Live in me from day to day,
By his love and power controlling
All I do and say.
(Kate Barclay Wilkinson)

Resolve to think holy thoughts.

Moreover, this verse, Philippians 4:8, is tightly tied to the next. After telling the Philippian believers to think holy thoughts, Paul goes on to say, 'Whatever you have learned or received or heard from me, or seen in me – put it into practice. And the God of peace will be with you' (4:9). In other words, Paul is returning to a theme that was very strong in the previous chapter: we are to emulate worthy Christian leaders. In this context, that theme is now applied to the discipline of the mind. In other words, we are to emulate Christian leaders who have clearly disciplined *their* minds. Of course, we have no access to a mind other than through what that mind says and does. But that is the point. Paul is saying, in effect, 'What was on my mind when I was with you? What did I talk about? What did I read? What was the burden of my conversation? What did I value? What did I do to improve my mind? Whatever you learned or received or heard from me or saw in me, put it into practice. And the God of peace will be with you.'

Resolve to think holy thoughts. This is foundational to the commitment never to give up the Christian walk.

Resolve to learn the secret of contentment (4:10–13)

Paul begins this paragraph by commenting again on the Philippians' concern to meet Paul's needs by sending support. 'I rejoice greatly in the Lord that at last you have renewed your concern for me' (4:10). The phrase 'at last' does not in this context carry derogatory overtones that blame the Philippians for being so slow, as if Paul were saying, '*At last*, you have finally got around to it.' Rather it means that now, in these last few days or weeks, after an extended hiatus caused by all sorts of things (not least Paul's constant travels), you have renewed the concern for me that you showed in the early days ten years ago. That this is what Paul means is made clear by his next sentence: 'Indeed, you have been concerned, but you had no opportunity to show it' (4:10).

But Paul very shrewdly grasps how his exuberant thanks to the Philippians could be misunderstood. Some people voice their thanks in such a way that it is hard to avoid the inference that they are hoping for another gift. Perhaps they grovel; perhaps there is nothing tangible in their thanks that you can put your finger on, but you feel slightly manipulated anyway. Once in a while missionary prayer letters sound this way; very often the thank-you letters from non-profit organizations sound this way. Perhaps. In any case, Paul takes no chances: he wants to distance himself from all of these possibilities, so he immediately explains his own motives: 'I am not saying this because I am in need, for I have learned to be content whatever the circumstances. I know what it is to be in need, and I know what it is to have plenty. I have learned the secret of being content in any and every situation, whether well fed or hungry, whether living in plenty or in want. I can do everything through him who gives me strength' (4:11–13).

This is a remarkable stance. Note especially two features of it.

First, the secret of contentment is not normally learned in posh circumstances or in deprived circumstances, but in exposure to both. Perhaps you have come from a well-to-do background, and you have never lacked anything. You have never had anything you valued taken away from you. The question arises whether you would be comfortable and content if you were suddenly forced to live in poverty. But on the other side, you may have come from a really poor background. Perhaps you learned to handle the uncertainty and the deprivation in godly ways. But now the question arises whether you could be content if you suddenly fell into wealth. Would it instantly corrupt you? Or would you feel so guilty with all these possessions that you could scarcely look at yourself in the mirror?

Paul carefully insists that his own contentment operates under both conditions: 'I have learned the secret of being content in any and every situation, whether well fed or hungry, whether living in plenty or in want.' He avoids the arrogance that is often associated with wealth; he also avoids the kind of spiritual arrogance that is often associated with poverty. The brute fact is that Paul is content in both circumstances *because his contentment is utterly independent of circumstances*. His contentment is focused on all that he enjoys of Christ Jesus. That means he has learned, by hard experience, a relaxed contentment whatever his circumstances.

Secondly, the secret of Christian contentment is quite unlike Stoic self-sufficiency. Paul is not claiming to be so strong that nothing can move him. Nor is he simply resolving to be independent of circumstances by a superlative act of will. Far from it: he immediately confesses that if he has reached this stage of contentment he owes everything to God: 'I can do everything through him who gives me strength' (Phil. 4:13).

This verse is often wrenched out of its context. Paul is not claiming to be a kind of superman because he is a Christian and God is on his side. His 'everything' is certainly not unlimited, as if Paul could be read to mean, 'I can raise the dead', or 'I can walk on water', or 'I can show you how cold fusion is a practical possibility.' By the same token, the verse should not be deployed by well-meaning but ill-informed church leaders who are trying to manipulate church members into doing something they really do not think they should do. 'But Mrs Jones, you can't say "No" to our invitation to teach ten-year-old boys just because you've never taught a Sunday School class before, or just because you feel you have no gifts or calling or interest in this area. After all, Paul teaches us that we can do all things through Christ who gives us strength.'

This is horrible. Paul's 'everything' is constrained by the context. His point is that whatever the circumstances in which he finds himself, whether with the rich and the powerful or with the poor and the powerless, whether preaching with unction to substantial crowds or incarcerated in a filthy prison, he has learned to cast himself on God *and be content*. He can do all these things, *everything* that God assigns him to do, through the one who gives him strength. Let the gospel advance; let God's will be done in me and through me, Paul is saying; I am content, for I can trust the one who invariably strengthens me to do what he assigns me.

It takes the strength and resolution and perspective that only God can provide to live above changing, difficult circumstances. But to live above circumstances, utterly content in Christ Jesus, is to ensure that you will never give up the Christian walk. Resolve to learn the secret of contentment.

Resolve to grow in the grace of Christian gratitude and courtesy (4:14–23)

These closing verses are full of wonderful pastoral touches. However much Paul is content regardless of his circumstances, he is grateful to the Philippians for what they have provided: 'Yet it was good of you to share in my troubles' (4:14), Paul writes. Indeed, they were the only Christians in their area to be quick off the mark in this regard: 'Moreover, as you Philippians know, in the early days of your acquaintance with the gospel, when I set out from Macedonia, not one church shared with me in the matter of giving and receiving, except you only; for even when I was in Thessalonica, you sent me aid again and again when I was in need' (4:15–16). It is helpful to follow Paul's course on a map. Paul left Troas in Asia Minor and crossed over to Europe, landing at the port city of Neapolis and proceeding immediately to Philippi. There he and Silas were beaten up, arrested, and eventually escorted out of town, but not before they planted this fledgling church. Leaving Philippi, Paul quickly passed through Amphipolis and Apollonia and arrived at Thessalonica, where in short order he started another church. So what Paul is saying is that even by the time he got to Thessalonica and began preaching the gospel there, before he left there to evangelize Athens and Corinth, the Philippians were already finding ways to help, and asking for information as to what part they could play in this great ministry. Apparently Paul stayed in Thessalonica only a few weeks, but during that relatively short time the Philippians came through again and again. And for his part, Paul is not slow to express his profound gratitude.

Once again Paul insists that his words do not suggest he is angling for another gift. If he wants anything, he says, 'I am looking for what may be credited to your account' (4:17). In other words, Paul is primarily pleased that the Philippians have been so generous in the work of the gospel, not because he has been the recipient of that generosity, but because by being generous they have been acting like Christians – and God, who is no-one's debtor, will reward them. He is more delighted with the blessings they will experience because they are a giving and generous church than he is with the help that has come his way.

Paul even tries, apparently, to redirect some of their future giving: 'I have received full payment and even more; I am amply supplied, now that I have received from Epaphroditus the gifts you sent' (4:18). In any case, whether the Philippians send such generous gifts to Paul or to someone else, the gifts were first and foremost offered to God: 'They are a fragrant offering, an acceptable sacrifice, pleasing to God' (4:18).

There are important lessons of Christian courtesy here. Examine how Paul thanks believers in his letters; read and re-read the opening 'thanksgiving' sections that mark all but one of his letters. His pattern is to thank *God* for what the *believers* have done or for the signs of spiritual vitality that he detects in them.

This is doubly wise. Contrast the opposed errors into which we easily fall. On the one hand, there are Christian leaders who are so unrestrained in their praise of people it is hard to avoid the conclusion that they control others by extravagant flattery. Of course, in some cases it is nothing more than a quirk of personality. I recall one particular professor who came to our home for a meal. He was famous for his fervent courtesy. In that meal we offered him lasagne or spaghetti and meat sauce – scarcely a high-class evening meal, but something we were going to have with the children that night anyway, and they certainly loved it. The venerable professor went on and on over the wonders of the lasagne: 'Mrs Carson, this is really lovely; this is an extravagantly glorious repast' – or words to that effect. But as this professor was known for his peculiar brand of hyperbolic courtesy, we took it in our stride. It was simply the way he was. But some Christian leaders, one fears, have adopted so generous a stance of praise for others, a stance that is then imitated by others around them, that their churches are no longer Godward. They are nothing but mutual admiration societies.

On the other hand, some Christian leaders, jealous for the glory of God and firmly committed to the belief that if any believer does any good in any way, it is nothing other than the product of what God is doing in them and through them, end up offering very few thanks. They are most begrudging in praise, their tight-lipped reticence their way of avoiding cheap flattery. Besides, they are so frightened of the sins of pride, their own and others', that they avoid the compliments that might turn heads. If you tell a preacher that his sermon was good, they think, he might strut like a peacock all week. If you were helped by the sermon, go home and thank God, but do not corrode the preacher with praise. Do not corrode anyone with praise – deacons, Sunday School teachers, church trustees, caretakers, organists, whatever.

But Paul has the matter right. He does not simply thank people (though he sometimes does that), he thanks God for God's grace in them – but he utters his thanks to God *before* the people. In effect, he approaches these believers and says, 'I greatly rejoice at the grace of God displayed in your life', or 'I thank God every time I remember you', or 'Your life is a fragrant sacrifice to God, a sacrifice with which God himself is well pleased.' That is precisely what Paul does here. He does acknowledge that it was good of the Philippians to help him (4:14), but he quickly insists that he is more interested in what this says about their character, and about what this will mean in blessings on their lives, than he is about his own enrichment (4:17). In any case, he insists, the gifts were first and foremost 'an acceptable sacrifice, pleasing to God' (4:18). And all of this excites Paul's rejoicing *in the Lord* (4:10), for he recognizes that the marks of grace in the Philippian church can be traced to the Lord Jesus himself. And meanwhile, he reminds the Philippians that, precisely because God is no-one's debtor, they can rely on him to meet *their* needs: 'And my God will meet all your needs according to his glorious riches in Christ Jesus' (4:19).

Even the final verses of this chapter reflect a Christian courtesy. 'Greet all the saints in Christ Jesus. The brothers who are with me send greetings. All the saints send you greetings' (4:21–22) – as if Paul is constantly trying to establish links amongst believers in various places. Then he smiles, enjoying the irony: 'All the saints send you greetings, *especially those who belong to Caesar's household*' (4:22). Paul may be in prison at Caesar's pleasure, but the gospel has penetrated Caesar's household. It is important to remember who is finally in charge, and how he works.

Resolve to grow in the grace of Christian gratitude and courtesy. By now it should be clear that this is not exactly like the gratitude and courtesy commonly associated with good breeding or good training. The categories are different; the values are not merely formal; even the forms are a little different. Christian courtesy, besides being merely courteous, strengthens believers, invites them to turn their thoughts toward God, multiplies the cords that draw them together as the body of Christ. Precisely because it will strengthen your own discipleship and edify your brothers and sisters in Christ, you will be multiplying the resolution of the church never to give up the Christian walk.

You may have noticed that I left out one verse: 'To our God and Father be glory for ever and ever. Amen' (4:20). This is not simply a formula that Paul feels constrained to drop into his text once in a while, without giving the words much thought. Rather, the apostle wants to remind his readers that even at this stage it is possible to pursue all the excellent advice he has provided in this chapter, resolving to be obedient to the apostolic imperatives, and yet somehow prostitute them all. The deciding factor is this: do these believers see that all of Christian discipleship, all of Christian virtue, all of Christian resolution, all of Christian perseverance, must be offered to the glory of God? Or do they think that these virtues are ultimate ends in themselves?

For the sad fact is that there are some Christians who will hear the injunctions of this chapter – resolve to pursue like-mindedness with other true believers, resolve always to rejoice in the Lord, resolve to be known for selflessness, resolve not to be anxious for anything but learn instead to pray, resolve to think holy thoughts, resolve to learn the secret of contentment, resolve to grow in the grace of Christian gratitude and courtesy – and they will treasure these virtues as little gods to be coveted. But that may lead not only to a new round of legalism. Even worse, these goals are simply not worthy of that much energy and commitment *if they are ends in themselves.* But if they are cheerfully and lovingly offered up to God – that makes all the difference. We resolve to pursue these virtues not *only* because they are good, but because God demands them and gives us the grace to live them out. And the result is that he receives glory.

What is clear from this last chapter is that Paul provides more than mere information, however vitally he construes doctrine. The apostle does provide ample information and knowledge, but he also leads his converts into wisdom: teaching them how to live as disciples of the Lord Jesus Christ, teaching them not only how to walk as his followers, but how to persevere in that walk to the very end.

Never give up the Christian walk.

Notes

1. 'Direct' is not perhaps the happiest term, but I cannot think of a better word at the moment. We might say that packing pork to the glory of God has *indirect* eternal significance, in that it honours the God of eternity and prepares me for eternity. But it does not have the same *direct* eternal significance that, say, fruitful evangelism or prevailing intercessory prayer does.

2. The Greek future tense commonly signals expectation rather than mere futurity.

3. James Paton (ed.), *John G. Paton: Missionary to The New Hebrides. An Autobiography* (Edinburgh: Banner of Truth Trust, 1965), p. 56.

4. The last few decades have witnessed the rise of another interpretation of Philippians 2, an interpretation that has found its way into many commentaries. I am persuaded it is wrong, and in any case I cannot deal with it here. One of the best treatments of the exegetical questions that are at stake is in the commentary by Peter T. O'Brien, *Commentary on Philippians* (Grand Rapids: Eerdmans, 1991), pp. 186–271.

5. As usual, I am citing from the NIV, but I would not want to mislead someone by giving the impression that I care nothing about anachronisms. At the time, of course, the English Bible that both I and my friends used was the Authorized Version: 'Be imitators of me, as I also am of Christ.'

6. David Peterson, *Engaging with God* (Leicester: Apollos, 1992).

7. A. W. Tozer, *The Pursuit of God* (Harrisburg: Christian Publications, 1948), pp. 45–46.

www.ivpbooks.com

For more details of books published by IVP, visit our website where you will find all the latest information, including:

Book extracts   Downloads
Author interviews   Online bookshop
Reviews   Christian bookshop finder

You can also sign up for our regular email newsletters, which are tailored to your particular interests, and tell others what you think about this book by posting a review.

We publish a wide range of books on various subjects including:

Christian living   Small-group resources
Key reference works   Topical issues
Bible commentary series   Theological studies